MASALA

THIS IS DEDICATED
TO EVERYONE
WHO THINKS THEY CAN'T —
YES YOU CAN

Indian Cooking
for Modern Living

—

Mallika Basu

MASALA

BLOOMSBURY PUBLISHING
LONDON · OXFORD · NEW YORK · NEW DELHI · SYDNEY

masala | məˈsɑːlə | noun

1.   A mixture of spices used in Indian cookery
2.   Someone or something that comprises a varied mixture of elements

This is an Indian cookbook for the modern kitchen; wholesome recipes with bold flavours that can be simply cooked and generously shared. It has easy cheats and useful know-how to allow you to create a true taste of India while leading a life filled to the brim with 'masala'. And it is rooted in a very real story – mine.

My story starts in Calcutta (now Kolkata), in India's eastern state of West Bengal, where I was born and brought up. As a reed-thin child with an intense dislike of mealtimes, my love affair with Indian food had an inauspicious start, certainly not in keeping with the love of food shared by the rest of the family.

Dolly Basu, my mother, was a star of the stage and silver screen; her feisty family dates back to the original Afghani settlers around Delhi. She would waft in and out of the kitchen in her kaftan to make sure our cook did her recipes justice. While she didn't enjoy cooking back then, she knew the exact theory of every recipe. Non-vegetarian curry, a vegetable side or two, ice-cold raita, fluffy rice and roasted papads joined rotis for an average weekday lunch. My fierce maternal gran, nani, was also a regular feature in the kitchen.

The real cook back then was my dad, a businessman from West Bengal with the aspirations of a chef. His weekends were devoted to magicking up elaborate feasts like meat biryani in a giant dough-sealed container, and raan, spiced slow-cooked leg of goat, served with all the accoutrements. We would often be joined at mealtimes by his dad, my grandfather Jyoti Basu – Communist Chief Minister of West Bengal, a veteran politician who was invited and declined to be the Prime Minister of India twice. He would enjoy chilli cheese toasts and spicy snacks with a measured drink, demanding for dinner 'something Continental', the Indian interpretation of European food, or meat curries so tender they barely needed chewing.

We were an unconventional lot. The food was always fabulous. And I grew to love it.

At the age of 18 I left home for university in England – merrily dispatched with the recipes for one tadka dal and one chicken curry. I quickly learned that 'curry' was the generic term used here for all Indian, Pakistani or Bangladeshi food, and that the dishes were mostly created to suit the British palate.

I embraced my new life, at first aided by ready meals, takeaway dinners and curry houses. But it didn't take long for me to realise that chicken tikka masala and Bombay aloo would never fill the gaping void that had opened in my life. I missed my family and ached for the flavours I had left behind.

And so it began. Along with a move to London (into an apartment with the half-Peruvian, half-British man who was to become my husband) and a Master's degree in journalism, I embarked on a quest to teach myself the recipes I remembered from my childhood. As motherhood, a full-blown career in corporate public relations and a hectic social life ensued, I continued to focus on becoming a more confident and creative cook.

Slowly but surely I stopped trying to replicate exactly the kitchen of my childhood, taking a fresh look at the flavours of the motherland. A modern lifestyle is all about time pressures and life choices; the Indian food I cook at home has to fit into this everyday reality. Many home cooks back in India face a similar conundrum – including my mother, who has evolved into a fantastic cook. And so I started recreating my grandmother's lovingly hand-stuffed potato flatbreads and a few favourites from my convent-educated aunty's seven-course lunches, knowing that I would do things differently – on my own, in my rather more minimalist kitchen. Drawing on the memories I have, and updating them for my own children.

Eventually, I quit full-time employment in favour of consulting and writing about food and never looked back. I turned my attention to writing an Indian cookbook that reflects the way we live today, a book that both respects the past and embraces the future.

ABOUT MASALA

In the pages that follow, you will find authentic recipes, both from home kitchens in India and from my own. Many of them are far more time-effective than you'd expect, thanks to some clever shortcuts and food hacks, but with absolutely no compromise on taste. I'm not ashamed to say that I love gadgets and packets; I'm happy to champion ready-made rotis and parathas, tins of ghee and shop-bought paneer, papad and pickle.

If fussing achieves a major taste benefit, however, then I will never take a shortcut. For example, it really is worth marinating kebabs and sautéing paneer before cooking it. The flavours I cook with are punchy and bullish, as they should be, and have been taste-tested by Indians and Indian food lovers. Many of my recipes do have a kick, but they won't make you perspire unless they are meant to — like the lamb stewed in an eye-watering quantity of chillies that was beloved by Rajput warriors (page 77).

My mother taught me that everything is good in moderation. Although perhaps that should be *almost* everything. I live my life by this adage and trust my common sense when it comes to salt, sugar and grease. Having said that, I don't ever deep-fry at home — really because I can't stand the sight of all that oil rather than anything health related! While on the subject, Indian food is not 'health food' but it can and should be wholesome and well balanced. There is more to it than curries — think lentil crepes, fermented snacks and grains galore.

So consider this book a capsule wardrobe of Indian cooking, with staples that never let you down and variations on main recipes that provide creative ways to surprise and delight.

The first chapter, Classic Curries, contains dishes that we know and love, for those times when you want something comforting and familiar. Quick Fixes speaks for itself; the recipes can be either meal-in-one or part of a more elaborate line-up. Slow Feasts features recipes that take time to prepare or cook but are most definitely worth it — royal projects! The Brunch chapter celebrates lazy mornings, because Indians know how to breakfast. Then you'll find Small Bites, with recipes to kick back with, including savoury nibbles and teatime treats, followed by Big Platters, with easy-to-assemble dishes for when you want to impress a crowd. The Side Dishes chapter has idiot-proof recipes for simple accompaniments, delicious dals and breads that are easier to make than you might think, for when you have the time and inclination to create a full meal.

You'll find recipes for ice-cold thirst-quenchers as well as warming, aromatic concoctions in the Drinks chapter, while the Sweet Treats are more than just post-meal desserts – they are moreish bowls and bites that provide much joy well after mealtimes are over. And finally, there are the added extras – chutneys and pickles that money can't buy and some kitchen essentials for when you're feeling bored or adventurous.

A comprehensive list of the spices used in my recipes, as well as other ingredients and useful kitchen equipment, appears in the reference section at the back of this book – it's worth a read before you invest in a gadget or fill your cupboards with spices you may never use. Indian cooking uses myriad ingredients and spices, for which I remain resolutely unapologetic. I hate the idea of ingredients collecting dust in cupboards though, so I have made sure that if you buy a spice especially, you will be able to use it in more than one recipe.

And finally, if any of your Indian cookery adventures end with a result that's more tragic than magic, the troubleshooting section on page 246 may help to explain why.

So, here is Indian cooking for modern living, from my kitchen to yours, for the many years of masala that lie ahead.

EATING THE INDIAN WAY

Indian food is traditionally served as a full meal with rice and roti accompaniments. Of course you can serve it more lightly or casually (tucked into a toastie, piled onto warm flatbreads or accompanied by a crunchy salad) but it is worth knowing how to go the extra mile.

Indian food gets its uniquely tantalising appeal from clashing textures and flavours. As a rule of thumb, take the 'opposites attract' theory as your starting point. If one dish is cooked with tomatoes, think about pairing it with a yoghurt-based curry. If one dish is explosively spiced, keep another chilli-free to balance things out.

Mix up the types of food to build a meal with a meat or vegetable protein and a vegetable side dish. Then add rice, dal or flatbread – or all three, depending on how intent you are on impressing those you are feeding. Be creative! Instead of dal, for example, you could serve the spiced chickpeas on page 47. Remember to think about how the dishes will look together, making the most of their natural palette.

Papads, pickles and chutneys are classic accompaniments for an Indian meal. You don't have to make all these from scratch, by any means, and in fact papad-making is mostly limited to a few more rural communities and regions in India these days. Pickle-making is going the same way, so experiment with shop-bought options until you find the ones you like best. Raita and drinking yoghurt also feature in our meals, often to douse chilli-induced flames or to aid digestion.

Each home in India has its own spice tolerance level. My dad, not content with the minimal amount of chilli used in our house, used to chase each bite of food with a nibble of fresh green chilli. Feel free to follow his example and serve your meals with green chillies, halved fresh limes and salt – but never put the chillies directly on a dinner plate, as it's considered terrible luck!

Water is always there on the table, but it is not usual to drink copious amounts of it, as this interferes with digestion (and does little to dampen any chilli heat). It's important to say that many families don't serve alcohol with dinner, or indeed at all. But mine has always enjoyed a drink in moderation, usually before the meal with snacks and nibbles. If you are serving alcohol with your meal, however, remember that simple is best: with all the complex spices in Indian food you want unoaked white wines, red wines with soft tannins, low-gas beers or spirits with mixers.

SERVING INDIAN FOOD

There is no such thing as an Indian 'starter'. Most dishes that are labelled as starters on a restaurant menu will really be street food or snacks. Depending on the number of people you are feeding, you may want to serve pre-dinner nibbles with drinks instead. When you sit down to eat, keep it simple and just place everything in bowls or on platters to encourage social sharing. Get people to help themselves at once so the food doesn't get cold. Once the meal is in full swing, ask everyone if they are eating enough and prod your guests incessantly to eat more food. These, together with the regular exclamation of 'But you didn't eat *anything*!' even when a guest has consumed three generous helpings, are cultural necessities. I wholeheartedly encourage this, in the name of authenticity.

Using your fingers to eat Indian food is particularly necessary when flatbreads are involved. My grandfather's standing joke following my move to the UK was that while the British taught Indians how to use cutlery, we taught them how to *savour* food with their fingers. There is some truth in this – the Hindi word *chamcha*, meaning sycophant, literally translates as 'spoon'. It refers to the Indians who were keen to adopt cutlery as a way to impress their British employers during the Raj.

The main thing to remember is to use your right hand; the left hand is reserved for ablutions and other hygienic matters best not explained in detail in a cookbook. Unless, of course, you are left-handed, in which case it's vice versa. The trick with rice is to swirl it with your curry or dal into a small mound, which you then lift into your mouth. Flatbreads are easier – fold and tear them and use the ripped piece to wrap up the food. As with most things in life, practice makes perfect. While it's not considered polite to lick your hands while eating, in reality it will delight most Indian hosts.

On the subject of post-meal etiquette, it's worth adding that rinsing your mouth with water is non-negotiable after a meal. It freshens the mouth and rids it of spice bits. When we were dating, my unsuspecting husband-to-be very nearly got struck off the suitable candidate roster by my horrified dad when he failed to do this.

THALI

The word *thali* means a 'plate', on which an entirely balanced meal is served with papad, pickle and a little sweet something. You can buy a thali with indents that act as inbuilt bowls; often a banana leaf is used as an eco-friendly thali that can be disposed of afterwards. If you don't possess either, fear not. You can create a makeshift thali by placing little bowls on a dinner plate or small round tray.

REGIONAL VARIATIONS

In truth, there is really no such thing as generic Indian food; instead there is a vast expanse of cuisine that is the food of India. While it is quite the fashion to choose imported quinoa and olive oil over indigenous millet and ghee in the upper echelons of Indian society today, traditionally our food has been driven by location, climate, agriculture, history, religion and culture.

The north of India enjoys more seasonal variations in temperature than the south does. It is the main producer of wheat, and hence flatbreads are an essential component of meals. With cattle-grazing land aplenty, dairy also features heavily. The foothills of the Himalayas also provide the perfect topography for growing the slender basmati rice, meaning 'the fragrant one'.

The south, on the other hand, has a wet and warm tropical climate with little seasonality. South India is the primary producer of rice, which features heavily in the cuisine there, along with coconuts, tamarind, curry leaves, mustard seeds and lentils. But while it's common to use the blanket phrase 'South Indian food', the southern states of India each have their own distinct culinary identity.

In the eastern state of West Bengal, where I grew up, the cooking is delicate and sophisticated. Bengalis are (in)famous freshwater-fish eaters, owing to the state's plethora of rivers and ponds. Turmeric and ginger, now lauded for their health benefits, and mustard oil feature extensively in Bengali food. Quite often these are delicately balanced with the five-spice mix panch phoron and fresh green chillies.

As for the west, the Hindu principle of *Ahimsa*, or non-violence, can be felt strongly in the state of Gujarat, the Marwari community of Rajasthan and parts of Mumbai. Orthodox and higher-caste Hindus there are also guided by the principles of Ayurveda, India's ancient system of medicine, which forbids the consumption of flesh, and also ingredients such as onions and garlic because they are said to increase the equally undesirable qualities of passion and ignorance. While street food is enjoyed across the country, Mumbai is really the go-to destination if you want to try some, owing to its affordability and variety in the 'New York of India'.

Traditionally, Indian families will cook the food of their region and community at home and venture out to restaurants to eat the food of other regions and beyond. As the word 'traditional' never quite applied to my family, we enjoyed a taste of many different regions at home, alongside our favourites from Delhi and Bengal.

USING THIS BOOK

Indians rarely write down recipes, deploying a time-honoured technique called *andaaz,* or approximations, instead. I've obviously steered clear of this by giving you more precise instructions, but please use your instincts as a cook and always watch what is going on in the pan. Look out for the change in texture, colour and aroma mentioned in the recipe. Remember that a little bit more or less of an ingredient isn't going to markedly change or even ruin a dish. If you don't have a minor ingredient, just leave it out.

The portions in this book are generous. It's an Indian thing. Cook a day in advance if you can: Indian food always tastes better the next day, as the spices have had longer to work their magic. Then savour the leftovers for a day or two. You can freeze curries, but not fish, rice, potatoes or sautéed vegetables, as they lose their texture.

Most recipes serve four and you can easily double, triple and even halve them. I have included suggestions for variations, and you are very welcome to create your own. Most importantly, have fun!

COOK'S NOTES

Measurements are given in metric throughout.

Some ingredients, such as liquids and some grains, also have cup measurements. For this I've used a standard 250ml cup.

Teaspoons and tablespoons are always level.

Hot water added during cooking is always kettle-boiled so it doesn't slow things down.

Oil is neutral unless otherwise specified.

Oil is 'hot' when it sizzles to the touch of a wooden spoon.

Onions, ginger and garlic are always peeled.

Garlic cloves are always fat.

Tomatoes are always ripe.

Yoghurt added during cooking is always at room temperature.

Salt is added 'to taste'.

Sugar is granulated white unless otherwise specified.

CLASSIC CURRIES

EVERY INDIAN KITCHEN STARTS WITH A SELECTION OF CLASSIC RECIPES.

The kind your mother bids you farewell with when you leave home so you never go hungry, and your mother-in-law teaches you to make so her darling son is taken care of. Inevitably, these are cooked with what my mother calls the 'usual masalas' – a spice selection particular to the region or community you hail from. Here curry refers to a sauce or gravy, although the word is often mistakenly used to describe almost any Indian dish.

This chapter pays homage to the popular restaurant classics and family favourites that will never fail to delight and will form the core of your Indian cooking repertoire. It contains all-time favourites you can enjoy as they are, tweak to your heart's content or use as building blocks to create more expansive meals.

My Home-style Chicken Curry, for instance, is pure comfort food if served with a bowl of piping hot basmati rice (page 162) and ready-made papad. But it can also be combined with Tadka Dal (page 172), Aloo Gobi (page 42), pickle and raita for a more elaborate spread. Similarly, Rogan Josh is just as impressive on its own or served alongside Matar Paneer Masala.

You will also find a few surprises. Here the ever-popular Saag Paneer includes a clever way to use up any greens in your fridge, while the Gosht Dopiaza puts oven-roasted onions to delectable use and my recipe for Bhuna Gosht can easily be transformed into another completely different lamb curry.

So take a fresh look at these evergreen Indian curry classics and relish the joy they will bring to your meals, time and time again.

SAAG PANEER
CHEESE IN SMOOTH SPICED GREENS

SERVES 4

3 tbsp oil
225–250g paneer, cut into
    2cm cubes
1 medium onion, roughly chopped
2.5cm fresh root ginger,
    roughly chopped
4 garlic cloves, roughly chopped
2 tsp cumin seeds
1 green chilli, chopped
½ tsp ground turmeric
½ tsp chilli powder
100g each of black kale, leafy greens
    and Swiss chard, washed well
625ml (2½ cups) hot water
1 tsp salt
½ tsp garam masala or a pinch
    of dried fenugreek leaves
Single cream, coriander leaves
    and lemon or lime halves, to serve

A perennial classic, paneer in creamy puréed greens (*saag*) originally hails from the north of India. I've tried this with many combinations of spring greens, cavolo nero, baby kale, spinach and more and the ending is always happy. The restaurant versions usually use spinach (*palak*) but whatever you decide on, the spices will lift the curry and make eating your greens an altogether more exotic affair.

Shop-bought paneer is just fine for this recipe. If you do make your own though (page 225), dry it well with kitchen paper before using. Keep fresh lemon or lime handy to squeeze over before you tuck in.

Put the oil into a pan, place over a medium heat and when it's hot, seal the paneer on all sides until golden. It will spit, so keep the pan loosely covered, using the lid as a shield to protect you from the oil.

Remove the paneer with a slotted spoon, then toss the onion, ginger and garlic into the pan. Cook for 5 minutes until they soften and start taking on colour, then add the cumin seeds, green chilli, turmeric and chilli powder and sauté for another 5 minutes.

Roughly slice and add the greens, along with 500ml (2 cups) hot water and the salt. Let the greens cook, uncovered, until they wilt, then turn off the heat.

When the contents of the pan have cooled sufficiently for your food processor or blender, tip the greens in and blitz to a smooth paste with the remaining 125ml (½ cup) water. (Or use a hand blender.) You should get a thick, creamy and bright green mixture.

Pour the saag back into the pan and place over a medium heat. Drop the paneer in, along with the garam masala or fenugreek leaves. Warm the mixture for 5 minutes until the paneer softens and bubbles start appearing.

Scoop into a bowl and finish with a swirl of single cream and a few coriander leaves. Serve with lemon or lime to squeeze over.

VEGETABLE KURMA

SERVES 4

15 whole raw cashews
1 × 400ml tin coconut milk (at least
    75% coconut)
1 tsp fennel seeds
4 green cardamom pods
2 whole dried red chillies
1 tsp cumin seeds
1 tsp coriander seeds
2 tbsp oil
1 medium onion, finely chopped
2.5cm fresh root ginger, finely grated
5 garlic cloves, finely grated
2 diced carrots, 1 peeled and diced
    potato, a handful of chopped
    green beans and a handful of peas
    (or use 5 cups frozen vegetables)
1 tbsp tomato purée
Salt
Chopped toasted cashews and coriander
    leaves, to garnish

The darling of hotels in south India, Vegetable Kurma is an irresistible curry combining creamy coconut and cashews with fragrant fennel seeds. In India, one of my favourite meals is an all-you-can-eat lunch or tiffin where this kurma is served out of an aluminium bucket. The bill is quickly smacked on to the table when you've partaken enough helpings of the food!

Speeding things up with bags of frozen vegetables is a boon in this recipe. With that shortcut in place, do take the time to grind your own spices – it makes a world of difference. You could add freshly scraped coconut to the curry if you fancy some crunch. Mop the thick sauce up with parathas or other flatbreads.

In a blender, blitz the cashews with a bit of the coconut milk until you get a smooth paste. That's your cashew cream sorted.

Next, gently warm the spices in a small frying pan over a medium heat for 30 seconds. When the time is up, leave them to cool, then crush to a powder using a spice grinder or pestle and mortar. You can remove the cardamom seeds from the pods, if you like, but I chuck the lot in.

Put the oil into a medium saucepan or sauté pan and place over a high heat. When it's hot, add the onion, ginger and garlic and fry for 5 minutes until golden.

Add the ground spices and vegetables to the pan, sauté for a minute, then add the tomato purée. Cook for a couple of minutes, adding a bit of hot water if the spices start getting stuck to the bottom of the pan. Then stir through the cashew cream and remaining coconut milk.

Lower the heat to medium, cover and cook the lot until the curry is thick and the vegetables are just cooked, about 5 minutes if you used frozen vegetables and 10–12 minutes if you used fresh. Stir in salt to taste and serve garnished with toasted cashews and coriander leaves.

MATAR PANEER MASALA
PANEER AND PEAS IN GINGER AND TOMATO

SERVES 4

3 tbsp oil

250g paneer, cut into bite-sized cubes

1 medium onion, roughly chopped

4cm fresh root ginger, finely grated

3 garlic cloves, finely grated

1 tbsp ground coriander

1 tsp ground cumin

½ tsp ground turmeric

½ tsp chilli powder

125ml (½ cup) hot water

1 × 400g tin chopped tomatoes

150g (1 cup) frozen peas

½ tsp dried fenugreek leaves,
    soaked in 1 tsp hot water

1 tsp garam masala

Salt

Coriander leaves, to garnish

2 tbsp soured cream, to serve
    (optional)

This dish of curried paneer and peas is a north Indian classic. Cooked in both Delhi and Punjab, it gets its distinctive earthy, tangy flavour from the combination of ginger and tomato, although if you ask me, it's the dash of fenugreek at the end that really sets it apart.

Home-style Matar Paneer uses fresh tomatoes but this version is favoured by curry houses, using a handy tin of chopped tomatoes. Gently sealing the paneer first prevents it from turning into crumbs in the pan.

Pour the oil into a large frying pan or sauté pan and place over a medium heat. When it's hot, seal the paneer pieces on all sides until golden. They will sizzle, so loosely cover the pan with a lid and use this as a shield to protect yourself. Remove the paneer pieces with a slotted spoon and then tip in the onion and fry for 5 minutes until it turns golden.

Next add the ginger and garlic and sauté for another 5 minutes until the ingredients are a deeper shade of gold.

Now add the ground coriander, cumin, turmeric and chilli powder, along with a few tablespoons of hot water. Cook this mixture, stirring, for 5 minutes until the spices lose their pungent smell. If the mixture starts sticking to the bottom of the pan, add a little more hot water.

Add the chopped tomatoes and cook for another 5 minutes. When the tomatoes disintegrate, lower the heat and let the mixture simmer for 2 minutes. When little holes appear, turn the heat up to medium and add the peas and remaining hot water. Drop in the paneer cubes, cover and simmer for 10 minutes, stirring gently from time to time.

To finish, add salt to taste and sprinkle over the fenugreek, plus its soaking water, and garam masala. You can add more water if you want a looser curry or leave as is for a moist, roti-friendly filling. Garnish with coriander leaves. If you want to turn this into a decadent version for guests, stir through soured cream at the end.

MACCHLI CURRY
SIMPLE FISH CURRY

SERVES 2–4

300–400g monkfish, cod loin or other meaty white fish, cut into chunks

½ tsp ground turmeric

¼ tsp chilli powder

½ tsp salt

2 tbsp oil

1 bay leaf

1 medium onion, chopped

2.5cm fresh root ginger, finely grated

2 garlic cloves, finely grated

2 tbsp tomato purée

250ml (1 cup) hot water

½ tsp garam masala

Coriander leaves, to garnish

Coated in turmeric and chilli and simmered in a gently spiced curry, this is a very simple way to enjoy fish with the lightest of spices. Fish in India comes from both the fresh waters of its lakes and rivers and from the sea. Although foreign varieties such as basa are gaining popularity in restaurants and supermarkets, the morning trip to the fish market for the catch of the day remains a firm tradition in the fish-loving states. In Bengal, for instance, this is traditionally a job for the man of the house, who prides himself on his masterful bargaining with the sellers.

Serve the Macchli Curry with freshly steamed rice.

Toss the fish with the turmeric, chilli powder and salt in a bowl and set aside for a few minutes.

Pour the oil into a wok or pan placed over a high heat. When it's hot, toss in the spice-coated fish and seal it quickly. Then remove it with a slotted spoon and return it to the bowl it was in originally.

Add the bay leaf to the oil in the pan and as it sizzles up, spoon in the onion. Soften the onion for 5 minutes, then add the ginger and garlic and sauté for another minute. Stir through the tomato purée, then add the hot water and bring to the boil, stabbing at the onions from time to time with a wooden spoon to get them to disintegrate.

Now, lower the heat to a steady simmer and tip the fish back in, along with the garam masala. Cover and cook for 5 minutes until the fish is cooked through and oil starts oozing through the surface of the curry. Garnish with a few coriander leaves and serve with steamed rice.

JHINGA MASALA
KING PRAWN CURRY

SERVES 4

600g frozen raw king prawns,
 defrosted (or use 460–500g
 fresh raw king prawns), shelled
 and deveined
½ tsp ground turmeric
½ tsp chilli powder
1 tsp salt
2 tbsp oil
4 green cardamom pods
1 large bay leaf
5cm cinnamon stick
250–500ml (1–2 cups) hot water
Coriander leaves and ginger julienne,
 to garnish

FOR THE SPICE PASTE

1½ tsp cumin seeds
3 tbsp oil
Pinch of sugar
1 medium onion, thinly sliced
5cm fresh root ginger, roughly chopped
2 large tomatoes, diced
½ tsp ground turmeric
2 tsp Kashmiri chilli powder or paprika
1 green chilli, finely chopped (optional)

Jhinga Masala is my variation on prawn *bhuna*, a spicy and smooth curry that has its roots in Bengali cuisine. The curry house method of cooking it often involves a pre-made curry paste – a far cry from the lightweight prawn curries enjoyed in Bengal. My recipe brings prawn curry a step back towards its origins and can be made with raw frozen prawns, which have been defrosted and cleaned first. While you would normally use mustard oil to cook this in Bengal, any flavourless, colourless oil will suffice.

First make your spice paste. Dry-roast the cumin seeds in a small pan over a medium heat for 30 seconds until warm and fragrant, then remove from the heat and crush in a pestle and mortar.

Put the oil into a pan and place over a medium-high heat. When the oil is hot, drop in the sugar and as it melts away, mix in the sliced onion and soften for 5 minutes, stirring regularly. Stir in the ginger and cook the whole lot for another 5–7 minutes until golden. Now add the diced tomatoes and cook until pulpy. If at any point the spice paste starts getting stuck to the bottom of the pan, add 2–3 tablespoons of hot water and stir to loosen it.

When the tomatoes have lost their shape, mix in the turmeric, Kashmiri chilli powder or paprika, crushed cumin seeds and the green chilli, if using. Stir through, then lower the heat to a gentle simmer and let the spice paste ooze oil. When it does, switch off the heat. (At this point you now have the option to give the spice paste a quick blend with 125ml (½ cup) hot water to create a smooth curry, or leave it with some texture.)

When you're ready to cook, clean the prawns and pat them dry. Mix the turmeric, chilli powder and salt into the prawns.

Next, pour the oil into a shallow wide pan and place over a high heat. When it's hot, seal the prawns quickly on both sides and remove with a slotted spoon. In the oil left in the pan warm the cardamom pods, bay leaf and cinnamon stick for 5 seconds.

Recipe continues on page 30

Pictured with Khichdi (page 46).

V

KING PRAWN CURRY

Now mix in the spice paste with 125ml (½ cup) hot water and cook until you see ripples forming on the surface. Toss in the prawns, along with another 125ml (½ cup) hot water and cook over a medium heat for 5 minutes. If you fancy more curry in the final dish, loosen with a further 125ml (½ cup) hot water. Garnish with coriander leaves and ginger julienne and serve.

TIP   This curry tastes even better the next day. You can also make the spice paste in advance and keep it handy in the fridge or freezer; simply warm or defrost it and then continue with the rest of the recipe when you're ready.

MURGH KORMA
CHICKEN IN YOGHURT AND SWEET SPICES

SERVES 4–6

4 tbsp oil

5cm cinnamon stick

2 black cardamom pods

6 cloves

2 medium onions (about 350g),
   halved and thinly sliced

4 garlic cloves, finely grated

5cm fresh root ginger, finely grated

1 tsp chilli powder

8 skinless chicken thighs and
   drumsticks

350g Greek-style or full-fat yoghurt

1 tsp salt

20 cashews, or 2 tbsp cashew butter
   (no added salt or sugar)

250ml (1 cup) hot water

4 green cardamom pods

¼ tsp grated nutmeg

1 tsp garam masala

Normally a curry house option for the faint-hearted, Murgh Korma is a yoghurt-based chicken curry that most certainly can involve a spicy kick. Mughlai in origin, it is cooked with cream and yoghurt in the dairy-loving north, while coconut milk does the talking in south India. Sizzled whole spices work their magic, along with a grand finale of sweet spices, added at the end to preserve their fragrance.

Don't be frightened of a bit of curdling when cooking with yoghurt — it's par for the course and it gives korma its characteristic appearance, along with the rich colour from the well-browned onions.

Pour the oil into a large pan or casserole dish and place over a high heat. When it's hot, toss in the whole spices. As they sizzle up, drop in the onions and sauté for 7 minutes. Next add the garlic and ginger and fry the lot for another 5 minutes until golden.

Sprinkle in the chilli powder and stir through for a minute, then add the chicken and brown for 5 minutes, stirring regularly. Remove the pan from the heat.

If you are using whole cashews, hold 2 tablespoons of the yoghurt back and give the rest of it a good whisk, then pour it into the pan along with the salt; if you are using cashew butter, add all of the yoghurt to the pan now. Purée the whole cashews, if using, with the reserved 2 tablespoons of yoghurt and a dash of hot water to make a cashew cream.

Place the pan back over a medium heat. Stir through the hot water, the cashew cream you made (or the cashew butter) and leave to bubble, loosely covered, for 35–40 minutes, or until the chicken is cooked.

Meanwhile, lightly bash the green cardamom pods, remove the seeds and then crush them using a pestle and mortar. Finish by stirring the ground cardamom, nutmeg and garam masala through the curry and simmering for 2 minutes. When oil seeps through to the surface of the curry you're done. Murgh korma is best enjoyed with naan or parathas.

MURGH MAKHANWALA
BUTTER CHICKEN

SERVES 4

FOR THE CHICKEN TIKKAS
6 skinless chicken thigh fillets
    (about 600g)
2 tbsp Greek-style yoghurt
2.5cm fresh root ginger, finely grated
6 garlic cloves, finely grated
1 tbsp ground coriander
1 tsp ground cumin
1 tsp Kashmiri chilli powder
Juice of ½ lemon
½ tsp salt

FOR THE CURRY
500g passata
4 tbsp soured cream
½ tsp chilli powder
½ tsp garam masala
75g salted butter
½ tsp dried fenugreek leaves,
    soaked in 1 tsp hot water
½ tsp salt
Chopped toasted cashews, to garnish
    (optional)

This dish is the mother of Chicken Tikka Masala. You'll find Murgh Makhanwala at every north Indian roadside restaurant or *dhaba*, as I discovered to my benefit while working in Delhi as a trainee journalist. Skewered chicken tikkas (kebabs) are first grilled and then nestled into a tomato curry laden with butter and double cream, which probably explains the enduring appeal of this dish!

Create that sublime, creamy texture here with a dash of soured cream, a chunk of butter and a jar of passata. The curry takes virtually no time to put together, so you can prepare the tikkas in advance and stir them through later.

Make the chicken tikkas first. You'll need four wooden or metal skewers; if using wooden skewers, soak them in water for 20 minutes before using to prevent them to burning to a crisp. Pre-heat the grill to high and line a baking sheet with foil.

Chop the thighs into cubes (4–6 pieces per thigh) and put into a bowl along with the rest of the tikka ingredients. Mix gently, then thread onto the skewers, leaving a small gap between each piece.

Place the skewers evenly spaced on the foil-lined baking sheet and grill for 20–25 minutes until lightly charred on top, turning them over halfway through the cooking time.

To make the curry, put the passata and soured cream into a heavy-based pan and stir well. Place over a medium heat, adding the chilli powder and garam masala and finally the butter. As it starts bubbling, remove the chicken tikkas from the skewers and tip them into the pan, along with their juices and the soaked fenugreek and its water. If the curry starts hissing and spitting, just loosely cover it with a lid.

Cover and simmer for 10 minutes until you see the butter oozing through the curry and the colour deepens to a rich red. Sprinkle with toasted cashews, if you like.

Pictured with Kachumbar Raita (page 180).

Palak Murgh (see variation)

MURGH MASALA
HOME-STYLE CHICKEN CURRY

SERVES 4–6
4 tbsp oil
Pinch of sugar
2 medium onions, finely chopped
5cm fresh root ginger, finely grated
6 garlic cloves, finely grated
1 tsp ground turmeric
1 tsp chilli powder
2 tsp ground coriander
2 tsp ground cumin
4 medium tomatoes, roughly chopped
    or 1 × 400g tin chopped tomatoes
2 tbsp Greek-style yoghurt
8 skinless chicken thighs and
    drumsticks (about 1kg)
375–500ml (1½–2 cups) hot water
1 tsp garam masala
Salt
Coriander leaves, to garnish

An ode to the comforting taste of home, every non-vegetarian family has its own version of chicken curry. Back in my fledgling journalism days in Delhi, the apartment caretaker Bahadur would cook this for me after my gruelling night shifts, deviously tweaking it slightly each time.

You too can tweak this recipe to your heart's content. I've included a variation below but you can experiment by adding a dash of cream or some almond butter.

Pour the oil into a large non-stick pan and place over a high heat. When it's hot, add the sugar and as it melts add the onion and sauté for 5 minutes, then add the ginger and garlic and sauté for another 5 minutes. If it sticks to the bottom of the pan, add 2 tablespoons hot water and scrape with your spoon to release.

Now add the ground spices and tomatoes. Stir for another 5 minutes and then lower the heat to a simmer, adding a dash of hot water if the ingredients start sticking. Cook the spice paste, stabbing the tomatoes and onions, until oil starts to ooze through the surface.

After 5 minutes, add the yoghurt and chicken pieces. Whack the heat up to high and seal the chicken, stirring vigorously to combine the spice paste and yoghurt. The raw smell of the spices should have given way to a lovely aroma that makes you very hungry! In another 5 minutes, add 375ml (1½ cups) hot water, lower the heat to medium and cook, stirring regularly, for 30 minutes until the chicken is cooked. When it's ready, the chicken meat will separate from the bone and a light film of oil will float to the surface.

Lower the heat to a simmer and stir in the garam masala and salt to taste. If you want more curry, add another 125ml (½ cup) hot water. Garnish with coriander leaves and serve.

VARIATION ➤ PALAK MURGH (PICTURED)
For a chicken and spinach curry, when the chicken has been cooking for 15 minutes, drop in 250g chopped fresh spinach or 6 cubes of cooked frozen spinach.

BHUNA GOSHT
EASY THREE-SPICE LAMB

SERVES 4

3 tbsp Greek-style yoghurt

4cm fresh root ginger,
    finely grated

6 garlic cloves, finely grated

1½ tsp ground turmeric

1 tsp chilli powder

1 tsp salt, plus a pinch

750g lamb chunks, trimmed of any
    excess fat

3 tbsp oil

Pinch of sugar

1 large onion, thinly sliced

375ml (1½ cups) hot water

½ tsp garam masala

Coriander leaves, green chillies and
    lemon wedges, to serve

Lamb chunks stewed in the most minimal collection of spices until it's soft can be irresistible — as this recipe proves. Here, the spices and juices from the meat come together with great affinity. The best meat to use for lamb curry is diced leg, but if a trip to the butcher is a tall order then boneless diced lamb shoulder or cubed neck fillets from the supermarket will do just as well. Leaving the lamb to tenderise for an hour or so in its yoghurt coating will work wonders for the end result.

Spoon the yoghurt into a large mixing bowl. Add the ginger, garlic, turmeric, chilli powder and the teaspoon of salt and stir to combine. Now add the lamb cubes and mix well to coat evenly. If you have time, set aside in the fridge for an hour to marinate.

Pour the oil into a large heavy-based pan and place over a high heat. When the oil is hot, add the sugar — this will caramelise and help to brown the onion, adding colour to the end result. Tip in the onion along with a pinch of salt and sauté for 10 minutes until golden.

Now add the meat along with its marinade and stir well for 5 minutes, browning the meat and cooking the spices. Add 250ml (1 cup) hot water, lower the heat to medium, cover and cook for 30 minutes. Sneak a peek now and again and give the lamb a good stir.

After half an hour, remove the lid and continue to cook for another 30 minutes. You may need to add another 125ml (½ cup) hot water to prevent the meat from getting stuck to the bottom of the pan. You want to end up with a thick curry that clings to the meat.

Stir through the garam masala to finish, and serve hot with the coriander, whole green chillies and lemon wedges.

VARIATION ➤ CHANA GOSHT
Sizzle a black cardamom pod and 2.5cm cinnamon stick in the hot oil with the sugar. Add 2 chopped medium tomatoes after you brown the lamb, and then stir a rinsed and drained tin of chickpeas into the lamb when you uncover it.

ROGAN JOSH
FIERY RED KASHMIRI LAMB STEW

SERVES 4

2 tbsp mustard oil
6 black cardamom pods
5cm cinnamon stick
8 cloves
12 whole black peppercorns
1kg bone-in lamb chunks
2 tbsp Kashmiri chilli powder
2 tsp ground fennel seeds
1 tbsp ground ginger
½ tsp freshly ground black pepper
½ tsp asafoetida
1 tsp salt
500ml (2 cups) hot water
250g Greek-style yoghurt

Velvety smooth and bold red in hue, this lamb curry hails from Kashmir, originating in Persia. *Rogan* is the red oil that seeps through the meat and *josh* means 'intense heat', so you know you are getting a fiery, richly coloured stew. This colour comes from either *maval*, the dried flower of the cockscomb plant, or *ratan jot*, the alkanet herb, which isn't approved for use in food in the EU. So we'll just have to settle for Kashmiri chilli powder instead.

There are two ways to cook this – the Hindu version uses fennel and asafoetida, while the Muslim version uses a garlicky shallot called *praan*. I'm sharing the Hindu version, which has virtually no prep. The lamb is simply stirred into sizzled whole spices and then stewed with ground fennel seeds and ginger and Kashmiri chilli powder. Needless to say, this is a great recipe for the slow cooker. Head to the butcher for bone-in lamb chunks, as they really add depth to this curry.

Pour the mustard oil into a pan or deep casserole dish, place over a medium heat and toss in the whole spices. As they splutter, stir in the lamb chunks and sauté for 5 minutes until sealed.

Now tip in the ground spices, asafoetida and salt and sauté for another 5 minutes until the spices coat the meat evenly. Add the hot water, cover and cook for 30 minutes.

After half an hour uncover and remove from the heat. Give the yoghurt a good whisk and stir it in, bit by bit, off the heat. Then place it back over a low-medium heat and cook, uncovered, for another 20–30 minutes until the meat is meltingly tender and the red oil is bubbling through. Check for salt, adding more only if you need to, then serve hot with steamed rice.

TIP   If you're not sure about the oil floating on the surface, cook your rogan josh the night before, let the oil solidify and then skim some of it off before reheating the stew. This is pretty sacrilegious, but if it makes you happy then I am prepared to overlook it.

GOSHT DOPIAZA
LAMB WITH DOUBLE THE ONION

SERVES 4

FOR THE MARINADE
2 tbsp white vinegar
2 tbsp Greek-style yoghurt
4 garlic cloves, finely grated
4cm fresh root ginger, finely grated
1 tsp ground turmeric
1 tsp salt

FOR THE CURRY
1kg bone-in lamb chunks
3 tbsp oil
2 whole dried red chillies
8 whole black peppercorns
2 black cardamom pods
5cm cinnamon stick
2 bay leaves
2 medium onions, finely chopped
2 tsp Kashmiri chilli powder or paprika
2 tsp garam masala
1 tsp ground cumin
2 medium tomatoes, chopped
125–250ml (½–1 cup) hot water
2 large onions, thickly sliced
Salt

The north Indian dopiaza is an intensely spiced curry that is steeped in onions and rich, dark spices, making it the perfect centrepiece for a special feast. *Do* means 'two', and *piaza* is 'with onion', so the name of this dish literally translates as 'double onion'.

Dopiaza has been popularised by the curry houses of Britain, but I first fell in love with it at the iconic BBQ restaurant in Calcutta's Park Street. So enamoured am I with onions that I once requested a *teenpiaza* (*teen* meaning 'three'), to much bewilderment. Homemade naan (page 175) is perfect with this.

Put the lamb chunks into a large bowl. Add all the marinade ingredients, mix together well and leave to sit for 1–2 hours.

When the time is up, pre-heat the oven to 160°C/Fan 140°C/Gas 3.

Pour 2 tablespoons of the oil into a large casserole dish and place over a high heat. When it's hot, toss in the whole spices, bay leaves and chopped onions and sauté with a pinch of salt for 10 minutes.

Now add the lamb with its marinade, the Kashmiri chilli powder or paprika, garam masala and cumin and brown for 5 minutes until well sealed. Toss in the tomatoes and 125ml (½ cup) hot water, cover and place on the middle shelf of the oven for 1 hour.

Just before the time is up, line a baking tray with foil. Toss the sliced onions in the remaining oil and spread out on the tray. Take the casserole out of the oven, give the lamb a good stir and return to the oven, uncovered. Place the tray with the onions on a shelf above it and cook the lot for another 45 minutes–1 hour, or until the onions start turning golden and the lamb is meltingly tender.

Take the casserole out of the oven and stir the roasted onions into the lamb curry to serve, checking for salt and adding more if you need to. You can, if you like, loosen the curry with 125ml (½ cup) hot water.

QUICK
FIXES

QUICK FIXES ARE AN INTEGRAL PART OF MANY EVERYDAY INDIAN MEALS.

—

The combination of several quick recipes adds up to a multi-sensory, balanced Indian meal that can be packed for lunch in a tiffin box (a tiered stainless steel lunchbox) or enjoyed by the whole family at dinner. In the Calcutta home of my childhood one meal was always being served while another was being cooked amidst the chaos of squealing children, barking dogs and highly strung adults. I still reach for the same recipes when Indian food needs cooking fast.

In this chapter you will find one-pot dishes to whip up for a speedy meal, as well as recipes you can cook quickly as part of a more elaborate spread. Spicy Sabzi Per Eedu, our version of shakshuka, is a great weekday lunch. Or you could make your work colleagues green with envy by boxing up Goan Chilli Beef Fry or Palak Chana and taking them with you to the office – they're both moist dishes without curry that travel well.

At the end of a long day away from home, these are the recipes to turn to for dinner. Spices play a key role here, as they provide an almighty shortcut to flavour. Most of the other ingredients in this chapter can be procured en route home if you don't already have them – tins of chickpeas, bags of frozen prawns or spinach, and ready-made meatballs.

For more leisurely cooking, quick fixes can be added to impress. Bhapa Maach makes quite an impact when individually wrapped in banana leaves. Other dishes, like Haryali Murgh, take little effort to prepare and will bubble away while you enjoy a glass of something cold with a friend.

So don't fall back on bland ready meals when you need to fill a hole fast; instead crack out those spices. Cooking Indian food needn't be time-consuming or complicated – the proof lies in the following recipes.

ALOO GOBI
ROASTED CAULIFLOWER AND POTATOES

SERVES 4–6

5 tbsp oil

1 tsp cumin seeds

1 tsp ground turmeric

1 tsp chilli powder

1 tsp salt

1 medium cauliflower (about 500g),
    broken into florets

8 new potatoes (about 300g),
    halved

1 medium onion, cut into eighths

4 garlic cloves, sliced

1 tsp garam masala

Mango powder or lemon juice,
    to finish

Coriander leaves, to garnish

Tossed in the lightest of spices and then tray-baked, this dish is a twist on a classic. Aloo Gobi was popularised by the movie *Bend It Like Beckham*, but it originally hails from Punjab, where it is enjoyed all year round, especially in winter when cauliflower is in season.

Normally, you would steam the potatoes and cauliflower first and then finish in a pan on the hob, but the oven provides a more hands-free option. Leave the cauliflower florets medium-sized so they don't fall apart while being cooked and turned.

Pre-heat the oven to 200°C/Fan 180°C/Gas 6.

Mix the oil with the cumin seeds, turmeric, chilli powder and salt in a large mixing bowl. Toss the cauliflower florets into the bowl, followed by the potatoes, onion and sliced garlic. Mix thoroughly, then line a baking tray that will hold the contents of the bowl in a single layer with baking parchment and tip the cauliflower, potatoes and onion in.

Roast for 40 minutes, stirring halfway, until the cauliflower and potatoes are soft and golden. Remove the tray from the oven and sprinkle over the garam masala. Finish with a sprinkling of mango powder or a squirt of lemon juice and garnish with coriander.

SABZI PER EEDU
PARSI-STYLE EGGS ON VEGETABLES

SERVES 2

4 tbsp butter or ghee
2 medium onions, thinly sliced
1 large tomato, chopped
2 medium green chillies, chopped
2 large broccoli florets, roughly
    chopped
20 green beans, chopped
2.5cm fresh root ginger, finely grated
2 garlic cloves, finely grated
½ tsp ground turmeric
½ tsp chilli powder
1 tbsp chopped coriander, plus a few
    leaves to garnish
80ml (⅓ cup) hot water
2 large eggs
Salt

This spicy vegetable sauté topped with soft, slightly runny eggs is a handy one-pan meal from the Parsi community of Zoroastrians, who left Persia over a thousand years ago and settled in the west of India. They brought with them a unique cuisine that combines sweet and sour – stewing meat in fruit and vinegar with delicious results – and a great love of eggs.

There are a number of variations on the Parsi theme of *per eedu*, or 'eggs on' – eggs on fenugreek leaves, on okra, on potatoes and even on minced meat. But for a quick and healthy dinner (or brunch) in less than 20 minutes, I can't resist adding a generous helping of green vegetables. Mop this up with warm bread rolls.

Heat the butter or ghee in a large frying pan over a high heat. When it's hot, toss in the onions and cook until golden, stirring regularly. This will take about 5 minutes.

Next, add the tomato, chillies, broccoli, green beans, ginger and garlic to the pan, along with the turmeric and chilli powder. Stir well until the tomatoes start disintegrating, then mix in the chopped coriander and hot water and cook, covered, for 5 minutes.

Remove the lid. There should still be moisture in the pan – if there isn't add another tablespoon of water. As talented Hyderabadi home cook Aarshiya explained to me, this will help the eggs cook slowly, absorbing the spices without burning on the bottom. Make two hollows in the masala (the back of a spoon is ideal for this) and break an egg into each one. Cover the pan again and cook for 3–5 minutes, depending on how well done you like your eggs.

Take the pan off the heat and serve the eggs and veg sprinkled with a few coriander leaves and salt to your taste.

KHICHDI
AROMATIC RICE AND LENTILS

SERVES 4

65g (⅓ cup) yellow lentils
200g (1 cup) basmati rice
5cm cinnamon stick
1 large bay leaf
Full kettle of freshly boiled water
1 tsp ground turmeric
1 tbsp ghee, melted
Salt

Khichdi, pronounced *kich-ri*, is rice bubbled with creamy lentils and topped with a generous swirl of ghee. Considered the ultimate soothing meal, it is served to the ailing or when a boost to the spirits is urgently needed. At its simplest, this is flavoured with little more than turmeric and ghee but here the addition of whole spices gives it a gentle lift.

Huskless yellow lentils, or moong, are often used to make Khichdi as they are gentle on the tummy. Red split lentils, which cook in the same amount of time, work well too. Khichdi has a particular affinity with fried, crispy things and spicy dishes such as Jhinga Masala (page 28).

Put the lentils and rice in a sieve and wash thoroughly under a cold tap until the water runs clear. Tip into a pan with the cinnamon and bay leaf, pour in 375ml (1½ cups) hot water and bring to the boil.

When the water boils, skim off any foam or scum that floats to the surface, then stir in the turmeric. Bubble this for 20 minutes over a medium heat, adding another 250–500ml (1–2 cups) hot water if the lentils begin to dry out. Stir occasionally to prevent the lentils from getting stuck to the bottom of the pan.

The cooked khichdi should be moist and runny in texture like a risotto, with the lentils soft and shapeless. You can keep khichdi in a sealed container in the fridge until needed; just add a couple of tablespoons of water when you reheat it. Add salt to taste then pour the ghee all over the top before serving.

VARIATIONS ➤ PARSI-STYLE KHICHDI
First sauté ½ teaspoon cumin seeds, 4 green cardamom pods, 4 cloves and 1 chopped onion in ghee for 10 minutes until golden. Add the washed lentils and rice to the pan and continue as above.

➤ MASALA KHICHDI
Turn your khichdi into a more substantial meal by bubbling it with a portion of Tamatar Masala (page 228), a large handful of mixed vegetables and ½ teaspoon chilli powder. Finish with ½ teaspoon garam masala and 1 tablespoon chopped coriander.

PALAK CHANA
CHICKPEAS IN GARLICKY SPINACH

SERVES 4–6

4 tbsp oil

1 large onion, finely chopped

2.5cm fresh root ginger, finely grated

8 garlic cloves, finely grated

1 tsp ground turmeric

2 tsp chilli powder

2 tsp ground cumin

2 medium tomatoes, roughly chopped

125ml (½ cup) hot water

500g fresh spinach (or use 10 cubes of frozen spinach)

2 × 400g tins chickpeas, rinsed and drained

1 tsp garam masala

1 tsp mango powder

Salt

A tin of chickpeas and some spinach, combined with a selection of spices, equals a wholesome one-pot meal in no time at all. If you want to make this even quicker, you could use a portion of Tamatar Masala (page 228), heating it through in a pan before adding the spinach and chickpeas and continuing as below. I have also used a bag of sliced mixed spring greens and a bag of baby kale as alternatives to the spinach with glorious results. If you don't have mango powder, a squirt of lemon juice will do nicely. Serve with toasted pitta or hot roti. *Recipe pictured on page 53.*

Pour the oil into a medium pan, place over a high heat and when it's sizzling hot, toss in the chopped onion and a pinch of salt and sauté for 10 minutes.

Add the ginger and garlic and sauté for another 2 minutes until the onions turn a darker shade of golden. Now add the turmeric, chilli powder and ground cumin and stir for a minute. If the mixture starts sticking to the bottom of the pan, add a couple of tablespoons of water and scrape it off.

Chuck the chopped tomatoes into the pan, stirring for a couple of minutes until they disintegrate. When they do, add the hot water. Lower the heat to medium and let the spices infuse their flavour into the tomato. If you're using frozen spinach, now is the time to cook it separately, according to the packet instructions. If you're using fresh spinach, roughly chop it.

In about 5 minutes, when you see oil oozing through the surface, stir the spinach into the pan, along with the drained chickpeas. Cook for a further 5 minutes.

Add salt to taste and then finish by sprinkling with garam masala and mango powder. Serve hot.

BHAPA MAACH
MUSTARD, CHILLI AND COCONUT FISH

SERVES 6

12 green chillies

12 tbsp wholegrain mustard

2 tbsp French mustard

12 tbsp mustard oil

150g desiccated coconut

6 × 125g skinless cod fillets
(or use 1 × 750g piece of cod fillet)

Salt

This Bengali dish is a fragrant and feisty way to enjoy fish. At its simplest it involves a quick marinade slathered onto a whole fillet of cod that is then baked, but you can lovingly wrap individual fillets in banana leaves for wow factor. The juices from the steaming damp foliage impart the fish with a distinctive taste.

However, fresh banana leaves aren't top of my mind on busy weekdays. So I am more likely to reach for baking parchment, or simply slather the marinade on the fish and loosely cover with some foil. I use cod loin, but this recipe works just as well with a slab of salmon fillet.

Pre-heat the oven to 190°C/Fan 170°C/Gas 5 and line a baking dish with foil or baking parchment.

Blitz the first five ingredients in a food processor or blender to get a thick mustard paste with a grainy texture. You could also chop the green chillies finely by hand and combine in a bowl with the mustards, oil and coconut. Once you have your marinade, add salt to taste. Now proceed with one of the following methods.

Place the individual fish fillets on the lined baking dish. Generously drench with the marinade and then bake in the oven for 15 minutes.

Alternatively, place a whole cod fillet on a piece of baking parchment large enough to generously wrap it. Evenly spread the marinade on each side of the fish, then wrap it up like a present. Use food-safe twine to tie up your parcel or toothpicks to thread the edges of your parcel together. That way the marinade will stay in place and your fish will remain moist. Keep the secured part facing upwards and bake in the oven for 30–40 minutes.

For fancier occasions, use fresh or frozen banana leaves (available in Oriental supermarkets) instead of parchment. Fresh leaves are better than the frozen variety, which can tear easily. A trick used in Kerala is to roast the banana leaf on an open flame to reinforce it before wrapping. You can make six small parcels and bake for 15 minutes, or wrap the whole slab of fish and bake for 30–40 minutes. Serve at the table unopened in the parcel for full theatrical effect.

MEEN CURRY
BAKED COCONUT AND TAMARIND SALMON

SERVES 4

3 tbsp coconut oil
1 tsp mustard seeds
1 tsp fenugreek seeds
15–20 curry leaves
6 large shallots, thinly sliced
6 garlic cloves, finely chopped
½ tsp ground turmeric
1 tsp chilli powder
½ tsp freshly ground black pepper
4 medium ripe tomatoes, diced
1 × 400ml tin coconut milk
    (at least 75% coconut)
1 tsp tamarind paste
500ml (2 cups) hot water
4 skinless salmon fillets

This heady curry, speckled with mustard and fenugreek seeds and curry leaves, is tangy, spicy and fragrant. *Meen* means 'fish' in both Tamil Nadu and Kerala; in fact the word 'curry' is often thought to have originated from *kari*, the Tamil word for sauce or gravy. At any rate, the southern states make some of the best fish curries (outside my home state of Bengal, of course, wink wink). This recipe, my go-to fish curry, has its roots firmly in Tamil Nadu. It is a particularly good midweek quick fix, as you can make the curry sauce in advance and just put it together with the salmon when you're ready.

Pre-heat the oven to 190°C/Fan 170°C/Gas 5.

Put the oil into a sauté pan or wok and place over a medium-high heat. When it's hot, toss in the mustard and fenugreek seeds and half the curry leaves. As they sizzle up, mix in the shallots and sauté for 5 minutes until soft, then add the garlic and cook for another 5–7 minutes until the mixture is pale golden.

Add the turmeric, chilli powder, pepper and tomatoes, stirring for 2 minutes until pulpy. Now, stir in the coconut milk. While it's bubbling, mix the tamarind paste into the hot water and pour into the pan.

Lower the heat and let everything simmer vigorously for 5 minutes until you can see oil oozing out through the surface of the curry. Get your salmon fillets ready in an oven-to-table friendly dish. Pour the curry over, scatter over the remaining curry leaves and bake in the oven, loosely covered, for 20 minutes.

CHEPA VEPUDU
PAN-FRIED CHILLI SEA BREAM

SERVES 4
5cm fresh root ginger, finely grated
8 garlic cloves, finely grated
2 tsp chilli powder
1 tsp freshly ground black pepper
1 tsp ground coriander
1 tsp ground turmeric
1 tbsp lemon juice
4 sea bream or sea bass fillets (skin on)
8 tbsp oil
Salt
Lemon wedges, to serve

Coated in a simple blend of spices and then fried, this crispy-skinned, spicy-fleshed fish will awaken the senses and, if you're lucky, clear your sinuses as well. When I travelled across Andhra Pradesh once, the restaurateur Khalil Ahmed observed quite accurately that this Indian state's food has three chilli levels – spicy, spicier and spiciest. But don't let any of this put you off, as you can adjust the chilli powder and pepper to match your personal spice preference.

I was lucky enough to learn this recipe from two expert chefs, Chalapanthi Rao and Abhishek Kukreti. Serve with a simple salad of courgette and carrot ribbons or Palak Chana (page 47).

Put the ginger and garlic into a bowl and stir in the ground spices, lemon juice to make a marinade. Add salt to your taste.

Now, use a sharp knife to make three vertical slanted slits (like a forward slash) on the skin side of each fish fillet. Slather even amounts of the marinade all over the fillets. If time allows, leave the fish to sit in its marinade for 20–30 minutes.

When you are ready to cook, pour the oil into a large frying pan and place over a medium heat. When it's hot, place the fillets into the pan skin side down and fry for 2 minutes, then flip over and fry for another 2 minutes. You may need to do this in two batches. Serve sizzling hot, skin side up, with lemon wedges on the side.

Pictured with Palak Chana (page 47).

JHINGA SUVA PULAO
PRAWN AND DILL BROWN BASMATI

SERVES 4

4 tsp oil

2 black cardamom pods

5cm cinnamon stick

1 tsp cumin seeds

2 medium ripe tomatoes, roughly
  chopped

½ tsp ground turmeric

¼–½ tsp chilli powder

200g raw king prawns, shelled and
  deveined

2 handfuls of frozen peas

2 × 250g pouches of cooked brown
  basmati rice

8 dill sprigs

Salt

King prawns, frozen peas and dill pack a punch in this wholesome one-pot meal made with pouches of ready-cooked brown basmati rice.

Brown basmati is a more wholesome alternative to white but it does take an age to cook and pouches are an additive-free, easy way round this. While each pouch claims to serve two, I could easily snaffle one by myself, so do bear this in mind when deciding your quantities. Serve the pulao with a pickle of your choice for a satisfying meal in minutes.

Pour the oil into a wok and place over a medium heat. When it's hot, toss in the cardamom pods, cinnamon stick and cumin seeds.

As they sizzle up, add the tomatoes, turmeric and chilli powder. Stir through for a minute until the tomatoes soften. Next, mix in the prawns and peas.

Stir through for a couple of minutes until the prawns are cooked through, then rip open the rice pouches and mix into the wok ingredients. Snip the dill up with scissors and stir this in with some salt to taste.

NARIYAL MURGH

30-MINUTE CREAMY COCONUT CHICKEN

SERVES 4

2 tbsp coconut oil

1 medium onion, thinly sliced

4 garlic cloves, finely grated

2.5cm fresh root ginger, finely grated

2 medium ripe tomatoes, roughly
    chopped

500g skinless chicken thigh fillets,
    halved

½ tsp ground turmeric

½ tsp chilli powder

1 tsp ground coriander

1 tsp ground cumin

1 × 400ml tin coconut milk
    (at least 75% coconut)

Salt

Everyone needs a quick fix chicken curry recipe for when they have zero energy and this fragrant coconut one is mine. While Indian chicken curry is usually cooked on the bone, thigh fillets are used here to speed things up.

Make sure you use coconut milk with at least 75 per cent coconut in it, to avoid it splitting and leaving you with tons of grease to contend with. Serve the curry with steamed rice, or the Egg Roast Appam (page 103).

Put the oil into a medium saucepan or sauté pan and place over a high heat. When it's hot, toss in the onion and cook for 5 minutes with a pinch of salt, stirring to prevent the onion from catching and burning.

Add the garlic and ginger to the pan, stirring for 2 minutes until the ingredients turn golden, then add the tomatoes and chicken pieces. Stir everything well for 5 minutes to seal the chicken; you will see the chicken oozing moisture and the tomatoes turning pulpy.

Now add the ground spices – the turmeric, chilli, coriander and cumin – and stir for 2 minutes.

Lower the heat to medium and stir through the coconut milk. Cook for another 10 minutes, lowering the heat to a simmer for the last 2 minutes. Add salt to taste and serve immediately.

VARIATIONS

> If you have curry leaves in your freezer, toss 10–15 in along with the garlic and ginger. Stir in ¼ teaspoon of tamarind paste for the last 2 minutes of simmering.

> Add halved new potatoes along with the tomatoes and chicken to give extra bulk to the curry and cook until tender.

HARYALI MURGH
BAKED CORIANDER AND MINT CHICKEN CURRY

SERVES 4–6

1 medium onion, roughly chopped

4 garlic cloves

2.5cm fresh root ginger

1–2 green chillies, roughly chopped

50g bunch of mint

50g bunch of coriander

250g Greek-style yoghurt

2 tbsp oil

1kg (about 8) skinless chicken thighs
   and drumsticks

½ tsp garam masala

Salt

Lemon or lime halves, to serve

Chicken steeped in fresh coriander and mint leaves is like the taste of summer in a comforting autumnal stew. *Hara* means 'green' in Hindi, so *haryali murgh* literally translates as 'green chicken curry'. This is very popular in the north of India, where fresh fenugreek leaves and spinach are also sometimes added, as is a dash of cream for a richer texture.

This version is a simple affair that requires very little by way of preparation. If you're feeling extra organised, marinate the chicken in the morning before you crack on with your day, then shove it in the oven to bubble away later while you get on with life. Hot rice and crisp papad would complete the meal beautifully.

Put the onion into a blender along with the garlic, ginger and chillies. Pick the mint leaves off their stalks and add the leaves to the blender, reserving a few to garnish. Trim off and discard the bottom 3cm of the coriander stalks and then add the bunch to the blender, again setting aside a few leaves. Spoon in the yoghurt and oil and blitz to a smooth paste, adding salt to your taste.

Now, make a few forward slashes on each chicken piece with a sharp knife and place in a casserole dish. Pour over the marinade to cover. If you are marinating the chicken in the fridge, don't forget to bring it back to room temperature before you start cooking.

When you're ready to cook, pre-heat the oven to 180°C/Fan 160°C/ Gas 4. Loosely cover the dish with foil and bake for 40 minutes, then remove the foil, stir the chicken well and return to the oven, uncovered, for another 20 minutes.

When cooked, the chicken will fall away easily from the bone. Stir through the garam masala before serving with a lemon or lime half and a few torn mint and coriander leaves.

GOAN CHILLI BEEF FRY

SERVES 4–6

1kg sirloin steak

2 tbsp coconut or cider vinegar

2 garlic cloves, finely grated

1cm fresh root ginger, finely grated

2 tsp salt

Flatbreads and raita, to serve

Coriander leaves and pomegranate
    seeds, to garnish (optional)

FOR THE MASALA

4 tbsp oil

2 large onions (about 400g),
    thinly sliced

4 green chillies, finely chopped

1cm fresh root ginger, finely grated

4 garlic cloves, finely grated

200g baby new potatoes, quartered

2 tsp chilli powder

1 tsp ground turmeric

1 tsp ground cumin

1 tbsp tomato purée

1 tsp freshly ground black pepper

Salt

Many Hindus in India avoid eating the Holy Cow, and its slaughter is also banned in several states following the rise of Hindu nationalist politics. But it's enjoyed by a vast cross-section of people, including Goans, Keralans and bad Hindus like me.

This recipe for steak sautéed with onions and chillies is easy to put together, despite its deceptively long list of ingredients. Normally, the beef in this recipe would be cooked in a pressure cooker but here the use of sirloin speeds things up, as it is quickly fried. While the new potatoes are optional, they do add heft to the dish and don't need peeling. Make sure you have warm pitta bread or rotis handy, and a raita.

Trim any excess fat off the steak and then cut it into bite-sized strips. Put the steak strips into a bowl with the vinegar, garlic, ginger and salt. Mix well and leave to sit while you prepare the masala.

Pour the oil into a wok and place over a high heat. When it's hot add the onions and sauté for 5 minutes until they start to colour. Then add the green chillies, ginger, garlic and potatoes. Cook for another 5 minutes until golden. Now add the marinated beef, along with the chilli powder, turmeric and cumin. Sauté the lot for 2 minutes and then mix in the tomato purée and black pepper. Cook until a fork pierces a potato easily – this takes 15–20 minutes.

Add salt to your taste and serve hot, piled on flatbreads with raita (the beetroot raita on page 180 looks especially pretty) and garnished with coriander leaves and pomegranate seeds, if using.

Pictured with Beetroot Raita (page 180).

PUDINA KOFTA
MEATBALLS IN A MINTED COCONUT CURRY

SERVES 3–4

2 tbsp coconut oil
350g lamb meatballs (pack of 12)
4 green cardamom pods
1 medium onion, finely chopped
4 garlic cloves, finely grated
2.5cm fresh root ginger,
    finely grated
1 tsp ground fennel
1 tsp white pepper
1 green chilli, finely chopped
125ml (½ cup) hot water
1 × 400ml tin coconut milk
    (at least 75% coconut)
5–6 mint sprigs, leaves finely
    chopped, plus a few leaves
    to garnish
Salt and freshly ground black pepper

Kofta are spiced meatballs. Traditionally, these are lovingly made by hand but on busier days, however, a pack of ready-made meatballs is just what you need (choose lamb meatballs without rosemary in them). Add a warmed up ready-made roti or two and that's a midweek feast sorted in no time at all. You'll never see a packet of meatballs in the same way again!

Put the oil into a wok or sauté pan, place over a high heat and when hot, add the meatballs and quickly seal on all sides. Remove from the pan with a slotted spoon and set aside.

Drop the green cardamom pods into the pan. As they sizzle up, stir in the chopped onion. Sauté for 5 minutes, then add the garlic and ginger and cook for another 5 minutes until golden. If the ingredients start sticking to the bottom of the pan, add a couple of tablespoons of water and stir to loosen them.

Now, add the fennel, white pepper and chopped green chilli to the onion mixture. Sauté these for a couple of minutes, then pour in the hot water. Bring to the boil, stabbing the onions with your spoon to help them disintegrate. Stir in the coconut milk and chopped mint and then drop in the meatballs.

Lower the heat to medium and cook until oil oozes out of the curry and the meatballs are cooked. This will take 20 minutes.

To finish, add salt to your taste and top with mint leaves and a sprinkling of black pepper.

VARIATION ⟩ Experiment with beef meatballs and a portion of the Tamatar Masala (page 228); heat 2 tablespoons of oil in a wok or sauté pan and fry the Tamatar Masala for a couple of minutes. Add 1 teapoon each of ground coriander and cumin, add 375ml (1½ cups) hot water and bring to the boil. Drop in the sealed meatballs and simmer as above. Finish by sprinkling with ½ teaspoon of garam masala.

SLOW
FEASTS

THE ELABORATE SUNDAY LUNCH IS A TIME-HONOURED INDIAN TRADITION.

Sunday lunch was strictly a family affair in my childhood home. The stereo would be cranked up with lilting tunes from classic Bollywood films and by the time lunch was served, it was nearly dinnertime. Nani would be casually inebriated, us kids prostrate with hunger.

This chapter is an ode to days of rest, when dishes are lovingly cooked and served. Black lentil Ma Ki Dal, for example, demands to be slow-cooked until it becomes buttery smooth, and a properly cooked Vindaloo Pulled Pork will fall apart when probed with a fork. Think projects, rather than recipes, which involve soaking, marinating and the happiest of endings.

Unsurprisingly, a number of the recipes here hark back to the regal splendour introduced to Indian cuisine by once marauding invaders. The establishment of the Mughal Empire in India gave us emperors who had fine tastes in arts, culture and food. This led to the development of an haute cuisine for which we can all be endlessly grateful today. My recipes for Badami Gobi Musallam, Mughlai Murgh Musallam and fragrant Gosht Biryani will ably demonstrate why.

Nestled alongside these are regional specialties such as Khao Suey, an Indo-Burmese noodle curry, and Jungli Maas, a dish of meat stewed in chillies favoured by Rajput warriors, all of which weave a rich tapestry of food history and culture. In my own home, the kids chop, peel and listen intently as I regale them with the stories behind those special recipes. Especially on Sundays.

So clear your diary. Invite the extended family over, stir slowly and savour the pleasure of the slow feasts in this chapter.

MA KI DAL

SLOW-COOKED BUTTERY BLACK LENTILS

SERVES 4

180g (1 cup) whole black gram lentils

4cm fresh root ginger

5 garlic cloves

4 tbsp tomato purée

½ tsp chilli powder

1 tsp ground cumin

Full kettle of freshly boiled water

1 tsp garam masala

50g butter

Salt

Soured cream, to serve (optional)

This whole black lentil dal is steeped in ginger, garlic and tomato and stewed for hours – an antidote to our fast-paced world. The name of this recipe was originally *maanh ki dal* – *maanh* is the Punjabi word for whole (rather than split) black gram lentils. That got shortened to *mah*, *maa* or *ma*, meaning mother. And this really is the mother of all dals. The ingredients melt into the lentils as they stew, with a drop of butter and some garam masala to lift the dish at the end. Do remember to factor in the overnight soaking of the lentils: it's a must for this recipe.

Wash the lentils in a sieve under a cold tap until the water runs clear. Then put into a glass or non-metallic bowl with lots of cold water, cover and leave to soak overnight, or for at least 6 hours.

When the time is up, rinse the lentils and put them into a large pan with 1 litre (4 cups) cold water. Bring to the boil over a high heat, skim off any scum that appears, then lower the heat to a high simmer and cook for 4 hours, stirring regularly.

Halfway through the cooking time, purée the ginger and garlic in a little warm water and stir into the lentils along with the tomato purée, chilli powder and cumin.

Keep stirring and adding 250ml (1 cup) hot water every time the lentils lose their soupy consistency. When the time is up, stir through the garam masala, butter and then salt to your taste. You can, if you like, swirl a couple of teaspoons of soured cream on the top when you serve this, ideally with buttered naan (page 175).

ORIYA DALMA
TEMPLE-STYLE LENTIL AND VEGETABLE STEW

SERVES 4

FOR THE DAL

200g (1 cup) split pigeon peas

150g butternut squash or
pumpkin, peeled and cut into
bite-sized pieces

1 medium aubergine, cut into
bite-sized pieces

3 new potatoes, halved or quartered

6–8 green beans

1 tsp ground turmeric

1 tbsp grated fresh root ginger

1 tsp salt

Full kettle of freshly boiled water

FOR THE TADKA

2 tbsp ghee

1 tsp sugar

1 tsp Bengali five-spice (panch phoron)

1 large bay leaf

4 whole dried red chillies

TO FINISH

1 tsp cumin seeds

1 tsp chilli flakes

1 tbsp coconut flakes

1 tsp ghee, melted

Dalma hails from the state of Orissa in the east of India. It is famously served to the Hindu god Lord Jagannath in the renowned temple in Orissa's Puri beach resort (I enjoyed many happy holidays with my politician grandfather there). Typical of temple cooking, where food is prepared by special cooks for festivals and worship days, it has no onions or garlic in it – they are considered un-sattvic in Ayurvedic cooking because they are thought to produce heat and passion.

This lentil and vegetable stew puts a very popular East Indian spice mix, panch phoron, to excellent use – do make the effort to source this or make up your own (page 235). You can mix and match the vegetables by using sweet potato, raw papaya or carrots instead of the squash and new potatoes. While you can substitute half the split pigeon peas for split Bengal gram, if you like, there is to be no further improvising with the lentils – they are specific to this recipe!

First cook the dal. Wash the split pigeon peas in a sieve under the cold tap until the water runs clear. Then put into a pan, cover with cold water and leave to soak for at least an hour and up to overnight. When the time is up, rinse the lentils again and then return to the pan with 750ml (3 cups) cold water. Bring to the boil and allow to cook at a rolling boil.

Keep an eye on the bubbling dal while you prepare the vegetables. If you see any foam rising to the surface of the lentils when you peek at them, scoop this off with a spoon and dispose of it in the sink.

Let the lentils bubble for 30 minutes, then mix in all the vegetables, turmeric, ginger and salt. Add 500ml (2 cups) hot water. Stir well and cook for another 30 minutes over a medium heat until the vegetables are soft and the lentils have cooked and incorporated into the liquid. They should be soft when gently squished between your fingers. Remove the dal from the heat while you make the tadka.

Recipe continues on page 68

Pictured with Dahi Baingana (page 69).

Put the ghee into a small frying pan and place over a medium heat. When it's hot, add the sugar, and as it caramelises, add the Bengali five-spice, bay leaf and whole dried red chillies. As they sizzle up, stir the tadka into the dal. Check for salt, adding more only if you need to.

To finish, dry-roast the cumin seeds in a small pan over a medium heat for 20 seconds, then roughly crush with the chilli flakes in a pestle and mortar. Toast the coconut quickly in the same pan to give it some colour.

Sprinkle the crushed chilli and cumin over the dal along with the coconut and the remaining ghee before serving hot. Mix the whole lot well before tucking in. This dal is perfect with Dahi Baingana (see opposite).

DAHI BAINGANA
CRISPY AUBERGINE AND SHALLOT RAITA

SERVES 4

1 large aubergine
1 tsp cumin seeds
6–8 tbsp oil
5 shallots, thinly sliced
¼ tsp chilli powder
400g low-fat natural yoghurt
Pinch of sugar
1 tsp Bengali five-spice (panch phoron)
15 curry leaves
2 whole dried red chillies
¼ tsp ground turmeric
Salt

Crispy, shallow-fried aubergines and caramelised shallots join spiced yoghurt in this luscious side dish from the state of Orissa. For Hindus this state houses one of the four Dhams, or divine sites, in the seaside resort of Puri. It is said that the Hindu Lord Vishnu, the preserver and protector of the universe, ate his meals there. A taste of the local cuisine will amply demonstrate why.

While there are temple versions of Dahi Baingana that omit onions, shallots bring a welcome sweetness to this dish. There is a good reason this recipe features in a chapter celebrating the long and the slow – there is no alternative for brining and then meticulously shallow-frying the aubergines. *Recipe pictured on page 67.*

Slice the aubergine into 5mm-thick discs and put into a bowl of cold water. Add a pinch of salt and soak for at least 1 hour. Meanwhile, dry-roast the cumin seeds in a frying pan over a medium heat for 10–15 seconds until warm, then crush finely.

Drain the aubergine slices thoroughly and line a plate with kitchen paper. Pour 6 tablespoons of the oil into a large frying pan and place over a high heat. Shallow-fry the aubergine slices for 3 minutes on each side until golden and crisp. They will sizzle as they touch the oil so shield yourself with a large lid!

Transfer the aubergine to the lined plate to absorb some of the oil. Keep going until all the slices are fried (you may need to add a little more oil). When they are done, arrange the aubergine in a shallow bowl. Then toss the shallots into the pan and sauté for 5 minutes until golden. Remove from the pan and scatter over the aubergine.

Now mix the crushed cumin seeds and chilli powder into the yoghurt, along with the sugar, a tablespoon of water and salt to your taste. Pour this over the aubergine (or serve the yoghurt separately).

Finally, warm a tablespoon of oil in the frying pan and toss in the Bengali five-spice, curry leaves, red chillies and turmeric. As they sizzle up, pour this tempering all over the yoghurt. Serve chilled.

BADAMI GOBI MUSALLAM
NUT BUTTER ROASTED CAULIFLOWER

SERVES 4

4 tbsp oil
Pinch of sugar
3 medium onions (about 350g),
    halved and thinly sliced into
    half-moons
400g Greek-style yoghurt
2.5cm fresh root ginger
2 garlic cloves
1½ tbsp almond butter
1½ tbsp cashew butter
1 tsp ground turmeric
½ tsp chilli powder
1 tsp ground coriander
1 tsp ground cumin
1 large cauliflower
2cm cinnamon stick
500ml (2 cups) hot water
1 tsp garam masala
Salt

A decadent centrepiece, this cauliflower is drenched in a luscious almond and cashew cream sauce and then roasted whole. It's the perfect feast for any vegetarians in your midst, and appreciated just as much by meat lovers. Blended caramelised onions add extra depth of flavour and sweetness to the dish, along with the nuts.

Rather than making nut cream from scratch, I prefer to use shop-bought nut butter, the kind with no added sugar or salt.

Pour the oil into a frying pan and place over a medium-high heat. When it's hot, add the sugar, onions and a pinch of salt, in that order. Sauté for 12–15 minutes until golden and crisp. Remove from the heat.

Pre-heat the oven to 200°C/Fan 180°C/Gas 6.

Transfer the onions to a blender, leaving behind 2 tablespoons for garnishing. Add the yoghurt, ginger, garlic, nut butters, turmeric, chilli powder, coriander, cumin and 250ml (1 cup) cold water and blitz until smooth. Add salt to taste. Pour this sauce into a casserole dish that will snugly hold the whole cauliflower.

Keeping the leaves on the cauliflower (they will char and add to the stunning appearance of the dish), slice off the bottom of the cauliflower so it sits comfortably. Use a sharp knife to stab the stalk end two or three times to help it cook.

Place the cauliflower upside down in the casserole dish, add the cinnamon stick, loosely cover with foil and shove in the oven. After 40 minutes, take the dish out of the oven, and remove the cauliflower with two forks. Add the hot water to the bottom of the dish and stir to loosen the curry. Return the cauliflower to the casserole dish, the right way up this time, and spoon the curry over the top. Loosely cover and return to the oven for another 20 minutes, then uncover and cook for a final 20 minutes with the garam masala sprinkled over.

Lift the cauliflower into your serving dish and pour the sauce around it, garnishing with the reserved crispy onions. You can also serve the sauce separately for pouring. Cut the cauliflower into chunks or slices at the table.

KHAO SUEY
COCONUT CHICKEN NOODLE BOWLS

SERVES 4

FOR THE NOODLE CURRY
2 tbsp oil
4 medium onions, thinly sliced
4cm fresh root ginger, finely grated
6 garlic cloves, finely grated
1½ tsp ground turmeric
10 skinless bone-in chicken thighs
    (about 1.25kg)
500ml (2 cups) hot water
1 × 400ml tin coconut milk
    (at least 75% coconut)
1 tsp lime juice
1 tsp fish sauce
375g medium egg noodles
Salt

TOPPINGS TO SERVE
4 eggs, hard- or soft-boiled
3–4 tbsp oil
1 nest of fine egg noodles, broken
1 large onion, thinly sliced
8 garlic cloves, sliced
4 spring onions (green part only),
    chopped
4 green chillies, chopped
Crushed dried red chillies
Shrimp paste
Handful of chopped coriander
Lemon wedges

Khao Suey is a curried coconut soup poured over noodles and then liberally topped with a selection of pick-and-mix toppings. A descendent of the Khao Soi enjoyed in northern Thailand and the Shan State of Burma, Khao Suey arrived in Bengal courtesy of trade routes that were established during the British Empire. Bengalis took to it with gusto, and each family puts their own spin on it – in a spirit of quite considerable competition!

My aunt Dolly Pishi uses lentils to thicken the curry, while my mother is partial to a drop of shrimp paste and my Bangkok-based sister uses Asian curry paste. My version features chicken on the bone, while the topping suggestions are there for you to explore and customise. Go all out if you have the time; the more toppings the better, in my opinion.

First make the curry. Pour the oil into a large pan, place over a high heat, add the onions and soften for 5 minutes. Add the ginger and garlic and cook for another 5 minutes.

Stir through the turmeric and chicken and sauté for 5 minutes, then add the hot water. Lower the heat to medium and cook for 30 minutes.

While the curry bubbles away get your toppings going, placing them in bowls one by one and setting them on the table. Set the eggs to boil while you heat the oil in a frying pan. Fry the broken noodles over a medium heat, removing when they are golden, and then fry the onion slices until crisp, followed by the garlic slices. When the eggs are done to your liking, cool, peel and halve each one.

Lift the chicken out of the pan and shred the meat, discarding the bones. Return the chicken to the pan and then lower the heat to a simmer and stir through the coconut milk. You should have enough curry in the pan to cover the chicken. After 5 minutes, remove from the heat, add salt to taste and mix in the lime juice and fish sauce.

Cook the egg noodles according to the packet instructions. Drain and put into large bowls, topped with the curry, and get everyone to help themselves to their favourite toppings.

MUGHLAI MURGH MUSALLAM
DECADENT WHOLE ROAST CHICKEN

SERVES 4–6
1.5kg free-range whole chicken
3–4 large eggs
Splash of screwpine essence (optional)

FOR THE MARINADE
4 garlic cloves, finely grated
2.5cm fresh root ginger, finely grated
Juice of ½ lemon
½ tsp salt
½–1 tsp chilli powder
1 tsp ground turmeric

FOR THE MASALA
20 raw blanched almonds, plus extra
    to garnish
150g Greek-style yoghurt
2 tbsp poppy seeds (optional)
4 tbsp oil
4 cloves
6 whole black peppercorns
5cm cinnamon stick
2 black cardamom pods
2 medium onions, thinly sliced
4 garlic cloves, finely grated
2.5cm fresh root ginger, finely grated
2 medium tomatoes, chopped
2 tsp garam masala
2 tsp ground coriander
2 tsp ground cumin
2 pinches of saffron threads
Salt

Roast chicken is resplendent on the weekend table at the best of times, but dressed in a sumptuous spicy marinade, it makes for a feast of regal proportions. Aptly, this version of Murgh Musallam dates back to the era of Mughal rule, when the Moroccan travel writer Ibn Battuta observed that it was a much-favoured dish in fourteenth-century royal courts.

Needless to say, this recipe takes time and has a long list of ingredients. But then, living the high life doesn't come cheap or easy to us ordinary mortals. Remember to factor in marinating and spice grinding time when you make this – both are well worth the effort. Serve with Zafrani Aloo (page 165) or turmeric-tinted Sabzi Pulao (page 164).

First marinate the chicken. Line a large roasting tin with heavy-duty foil (use two layers if necessary), leaving enough foil around the edges to securely wrap the chicken. Place the chicken in the middle and use a sharp knife to make incisions in the chicken at regular intervals.

Mix all the marinade ingredients together in a bowl. Slather the marinade all over the chicken and wrap in the foil, sealing it well. Leave in the fridge overnight.

When you're ready to start cooking, take the chicken out of the fridge and bring it back to room temperature while you make the masala.

Blitz the almonds with the yoghurt and poppy seeds, if using, into a thick cream and set aside. Pour the oil into a medium pan and place over a high heat. When hot, toss in the cloves, peppercorns, cinnamon stick and cardamom pods. As they sizzle up, add the sliced onions and sauté for 5 minutes until coloured, then add the garlic and ginger and cook for another 10 minutes until golden.

Now add the tomatoes, garam masala, coriander and cumin. Cook this for another 5 minutes over a high heat, then lower the heat and simmer until oil oozes to the surface.

    Recipe continues on page 76

Pictured with Zafrani Aloo (page 165).

Stir the almond cream through the masala and cook for another
5 minutes, stirring regularly, until you see oil oozing out again and
the colour returns. You want a thick coating for the chicken! Stir
in the saffron and add salt to your taste – a teaspoon should be
sufficient. Remove from the heat and set aside to cool. Meanwhile,
pre-heat the oven to 190°C/Fan 170°C/Gas 5.

When the masala is cool enough to handle, uncover the chicken by
carefully opening up the foil. Smother the chicken with the masala,
reseal tightly with the same foil and place in the oven for 1 hour.

When the hour is up, take the chicken out of the oven and open the
foil carefully to baste it with the juices collecting on the bottom of
the foil, then loosely seal it up again. Return to the oven for another
30 minutes.

Place the eggs in a pan of cold water, bring to the boil and let
them bubble for 6–8 minutes. Rinse them under a cold tap and peel
them gently.

Place the chicken on a platter, pouring the juices over it. Garnish
with the eggs and the remaining almonds, roughly chopped. Finish
with a splash of screwpine essence, if using.

JUNGLI MAAS
LAMB STEWED IN CHILLIES AND GARLIC

SERVES 4–6
50g whole dried red chillies
250g whole garlic cloves
    (about 8–10 bulbs)
4 tbsp ghee
1kg bone-in lamb chunks
1 tsp salt

Jungli Maas, meaning wild or jungle meat, is a moreish and mouth-numbing stew made with little more than sizzling hot whole dried red chillies and a generous amount of garlic. It originated from the hunting trips of Rajasthan's famous Rajputs, the Hindu warrior caste. Their cooks carried minimal ingredients with which to cook the spoils of the kill, usually game meat. Red chillies cleansed the meat and masked the strong gamey smell as it slow-cooked over the campfire.

My father would cook this lamb version for hours over a slow heat, with regular sprinkling of hot water and ghee. But Boobie, my half-Rajput friend and an amazing cook, helped perfect the time-efficient method given here, with a succulent end result, and homemade ghee (page 224) elevates it to new levels. As this dish may promote much chilli-inspired bravado, keep some cooling yoghurt and a fire extinguisher handy.

Soak the whole dried red chillies in a bowl of cold water; this will help release some of the seeds. While they are soaking, peel the garlic cloves and pre-heat the oven to 190°C/Fan 170°C/Gas 5.

Put the ghee into a large casserole dish and place over a high heat. When it's hot, toss in the garlic cloves and coat with the ghee. As they start to colour, mix in the lamb pieces and salt. Brown the lamb for 2 minutes, stirring quickly, until the meat starts to release some water. Scoop the red chillies out of the bowl, squeezing out the excess water, and add them to the casserole dish.

Stir through well, then cover and bake in the oven for 40 minutes, stirring once halfway through. Remove the lid, stir again and bake uncovered for another 20 minutes, stirring halfway through cooking.

VARIATION ➤ HIRAN KA JUNGLI MAAS
Do as the hunters did and make this with 1kg diced venison haunch. Roast the meat covered for 45 minutes, stirring once, and then uncovered for another 30 minutes.

KASHMIRI KOFTA
GINGER AND FENNEL MEATBALLS

SERVES 4

FOR THE MEATBALLS
1 black cardamom pod
1 tsp garam masala
1 tsp Kashmiri chilli powder
1 tsp ground fennel
1 tsp ground ginger
1 tsp ground coriander
1 tsp ground cumin
½ tsp asafoetida
500g good-quality lamb mince
1 tbsp Greek-style yoghurt
1 tsp salt

FOR THE CURRY
2 tbsp mustard oil
Pinch of asafoetida
2 black cardamom pods
8 cloves
2 tsp ground fennel
2 tsp ground ginger
1 tbsp Kashmiri chilli powder
250ml (1 cup) hot water
½ tsp garam masala
Salt
Coriander leaves, to garnish
   (optional)

Kashmiri Kofta, or *mutsch*, are pillowy-soft lamb meatballs simmered in the region's favoured spices. Two Kashmiris waded in with advice on this recipe – food blogger Anita and Mr Raina, my mother's friend and a keen cook.

'Meatball' is a bit of a misnomer because the mince is shaped more like a sausage. The quality of the lamb is everything – it should contain less than 10 per cent fat. Traditionally the meatballs are simmered on the hob but I bake them in the oven for ease. You need little more than steamed rice and a fresh salad to go with this feast.

First make your meatballs. Lightly bash the black cardamom pod to remove the seeds and then grind them finely using a pestle and mortar. Tip the powder into a large bowl along with the other ground spices, the lamb mince, yoghurt and salt. Use your hands to squeeze the ingredients together until the mince and spices are well combined.

Divide the spiced lamb mince into 12 even portions. Get a metal plate or tray and turn it upside down. Take a lump of lamb and roll it into a sausage shape on the metal plate or tray. This helps tighten and smooth the mince and create the shape. You want them to look like fingers, as the middles will swell when they cook. Place each one in a shallow, ovenproof dish large enough to accommodate them comfortably, loosely cover with cling film and chill for an hour.

When you're ready to cook, pre-heat the oven to 190°C/Fan 170°C/Gas 5.

To make the curry, pour the oil into a frying pan and place over a medium heat. When it's hot, add the asafoetida, black cardamom pods, cloves, fennel, ginger and chilli powder. Stir well, then add the hot water and bring to the boil. Add salt to taste.

Remove the meatballs from the fridge and pour the bubbling curry over them. Shove into the oven and cook, uncovered, for 40 minutes until dark and sizzling, turning once or twice during cooking. Sprinkle the garam masala over and stir through gently before serving, garnished with coriander leaves, if liked.

SIKANDARI RAAN
ROASTED MARINATED LEG OF LAMB

SERVES 4–6
1.25–1.5kg leg of lamb
1 tbsp oil
1 medium onion, thinly sliced
Pinch of sugar
Pinch of salt
2 tbsp toasted cashews, to garnish

FOR THE MARINADE
2.5cm cinnamon stick
2 medium bay leaves
1½ tsp cumin seeds
1½ tsp coriander seeds
1 whole dried red chilli
1 mace blade
¼ tsp grated nutmeg
2 black cardamom pods
4 green cardamom pods
1 large onion, roughly chopped
6 garlic cloves, finely grated
2.5cm fresh root ginger,
    finely grated
1 tsp poppy seeds (optional)
125g Greek-style yoghurt
1 tsp salt

For a Sunday roast with a difference, you can't beat the majestic Sikandari Raan. The name translates as 'Alexander's lamb' and it is cooked as part of the feast to celebrate Alexander the Great's conquest of India. *Raan* means 'leg' and traditionally this was made with the slow-cooked hind leg of a goat that was then finished off in the tandoor.

My version has a curry sauce to spoon over, the result of feedback from friends and family after many a Sunday lunch. Beyond that, Raan needs little more than Kachumbar Raita (page 180) and some rice, but you could go all out and make the Ma Ki Dal (page 64) to accompany this too.

First make the marinade. Warm the cinnamon stick, bay leaves, cumin and coriander seeds, dried red chilli, mace flower, nutmeg and black and green cardamom pods in a dry frying pan over a medium heat for 30 seconds until their roasted aroma starts wafting into the kitchen. Shake the pan gently to make sure they roast evenly. Turn off the heat and leave to rest in the pan.

Put the cooled spices into a blender or food processor with all the remaining marinade ingredients and blitz. You may want to add a tablespoon or two of hot water to get a smooth paste.

Line a large baking tray with foil and place the lamb on top. Poke the joint at regular intervals with the tip of a sharp knife, then slather the marinade all over the joint, working it in with your hands. Seal the tray well with more foil and leave the lamb to marinate like this in the fridge for 1–4 hours, overnight if you can. Turn once during this time, carefully unwrapping and rewrapping the joint when you do.

When you're ready to cook, bring the lamb to room temperature while you pre-heat the oven to 160°C/Fan 140°C/Gas 3.

Gently unwrap the lamb and carefully pour 250ml (1 cup) cold water into the bottom of the tray (you don't want to wash the marinade off), then cover again and roast in the middle of the oven for 2½ hours.

   Recipe continues on page 82

When the time is up, remove the foil cover and set aside for later. Spoon the curry at the bottom of the pan over the lamb, then increase the heat to 200°C/Fan 180°C/Gas 6 and return to the oven for another 30 minutes to brown the lamb, basting it once with the juices in the tray during this time. Don't worry if the yoghurt has separated; this is all par for the course.

Meanwhile, put the oil into a frying pan and place over a high heat. Add the sliced onion with the pinch of sugar and salt and fry for 15 minutes until golden and crisp. Remove with a slotted spoon and set aside on some kitchen paper.

Take the lamb out of the oven, place on a serving plate and leave to rest, covered with the foil you set aside earlier. Pour the curry at the bottom of the tray into the pan you fried the onions in and simmer gently for 5 minutes until it darkens. Skim off any excess oil and then pour into a bowl or jug, which you can pass around your lucky diners.

Serve the lamb with the crisp onions, the toasted cashews sprinkled on top and the jug of curry on the side.

GOSHT BIRYANI
FRAGRANT LAYERED RICE AND LAMB

SERVES 4–6

FOR THE BIRYANI MASALA
4 black and 4 green cardamom pods
5cm cinnamon stick
4 cloves
1 tsp white pepper
8 whole black peppercorns
2 tsp cumin seeds
1 tbsp coriander seeds
4 mace blades
½ nutmeg

FOR THE MEAT
4 tbsp oil
4 large onions, halved and thinly sliced
8 garlic cloves, finely grated
2.5cm fresh root ginger, finely grated
½ tsp chilli powder
1kg bone-in lamb chunks
4 tbsp Greek-style yoghurt
250ml (1 cup) hot water
Salt

FOR THE RICE
500g long-grain basmati rice
2 black cardamom pods
2 bay leaves
5cm cinnamon stick
4 cloves
1.1 litres (4½ cups) hot water
2½ tsp salt

TO FINISH
1 large onion, thinly sliced
1½ tbsp oil
3 tbsp whole milk
3 pinches of saffron threads
2 tbsp ghee
1 tbsp screwpine essence
2 tsp rose water

This layered rice and lamb feast, filled with heady aromatic spices and floral essences, was turned into an art form in the courts of India's Mughal emperors, and there are different versions in every part of India that was touched by them. Mine is inspired by the biryani cooked by my father and, more recently, my childhood friend Sanchita, who sent me her recipe, one line at a time, on WhatsApp.

There's no such thing as a quick biryani. A *kacchi*, or biryani that is assembled with uncooked meat and rice, is slow-cooked in a sealed container or *dum pukht* and can take 4–6 hours from start to finish. Even the family-friendly version below requires you to clear the decks for at least 3 hours – possibly more if you count the restorative sleep you may need after it.

Place the biryani masala ingredients in a warm frying pan and gently toast for a minute over a medium heat. Set aside to cool then grind into a fine powder in a spice grinder (or use a pestle and mortar).

Now make a start on the lamb. Pour the oil into a large pan and place over a high heat. When it's hot, toss in the sliced onions and sauté for 10 minutes until they start to colour. Add the garlic and ginger and cook for 5 minutes, stirring regularly. Mix in 2 tablespoons of the biryani masala (any left over can be kept and used as garam masala) and the chilli powder, then toss in the lamb pieces. Stir the whole lot thoroughly, browning the meat for 10 minutes.

Stir in the yoghurt and salt to taste. Add the water, cover and cook over a medium-high heat for 1 hour. You'll need to keep an eye on the curry, stirring it regularly to make sure it doesn't stick to the pan.

Prepare the rice. Place the basmati in a sieve and wash it thoroughly under the cold tap until the water runs clear. Tip the rice into a bowl, cover with cold water and leave to soak for half an hour.

While that's soaking, caramelise the sliced onion for the garnish by frying in the oil over a medium-high heat. Warm the milk in a small pan over a low heat and drop the saffron in it to infuse.

Recipe continues on page 85

When the time is up on the rice, drain it in a sieve, give it another rinse and then tip it into a large pan. Add the cardamom pods, bay leaves, cinnamon stick, cloves, hot water and salt, stir through once with a fork and bring the rice to a rapid boil over a high heat. Lower the heat to a simmer, cover and cook for 8 minutes, then drain and tip it back into the pan it was cooked in. Stir it once with a fork and leave to sit uncovered. You can pick out the whole spices if you want, but they do have more life left in them so I usually leave them in to infuse the rice even further.

Uncover the meat and cook off any extra liquid in the pan, leaving a thick onion paste that clings to the meat and oozes oil. Test a piece of the meat to make sure it's soft. If it isn't, keep cooking it for another 15 minutes, adding a few tablespoons of water to prevent the meat from drying out.

When the meat is done, it's time to assemble the biryani. Pre-heat the oven to 180°C/Fan 160°C/Gas 4. Rub a tablespoon of the ghee onto the base of a heavy casserole or deep ovenproof dish with a tight-fitting lid, big enough to snugly accommodate the ingredients.

Spread half the rice evenly over the base of the casserole dish. Skim the oil off the meat and spoon it on top of the rice, along with a tablespoon of the milk and saffron mixture. Place the meat on the rice in a single layer, along with its curry. Spread the remaining rice on top, dot with the remaining ghee, swirl over the floral essences and the remaining milk and saffron. Spread the caramelised onion on top and seal the whole lot with foil and then add the lid. I also put an upturned heavy roasting tin on the top just to make sure no steam escapes.

Place the whole contraption on the middle shelf of the oven and cook for 10 minutes. Bring it to the table and unveil it in its full glory.

VINDALOO PULLED PORK

SERVES 4–6
1.2–1.3kg boneless pork
    shoulder joint
2 medium onions, thinly sliced
4 tbsp oil
½ tsp salt

FOR THE VINDALOO PASTE
16 dried red Kashmiri chillies
2–4 whole dried red chillies
2 tsp cumin seeds
10cm cinnamon stick
8 whole black peppercorns
8 cloves
8 large garlic cloves
2.5cm fresh root ginger
4 tbsp coconut or
    apple cider vinegar
1 tsp tamarind paste
2 tsp soft light brown sugar
1 tsp ground turmeric
Salt

Fiery, sour and sweet, vindaloo nods to Goa's Portuguese heritage. Vindaloo literally translates as 'wine' (*vinha*) and 'garlic' (*a'hlos*). Despite its Portuguese origin, the Indian love for chillies and our indigenous ingredients slowly made their way into the dish. Bengalis cook it too, as a result of a brief fling with Portuguese colonialists; so irresistible is this dish that the Parsi community have also adopted it.

I roped in my American friend Adam to help work out how to make pulled pork with vindaloo paste. The result is a fork-shredded feast that is just as good tucked into a bun as with steamed rice and a Parsi Coconut Dal (page 174) and some yoghurt to balance out the heat. While vindaloo should be fiery, it is not meant to blow your head off, so adjust the chillies accordingly. *Recipe pictured overleaf.*

First make the vindaloo paste. Put the dried chillies, cumin seeds, cinnamon stick, peppercorns and cloves into a warm frying pan and dry-roast over a medium heat, gently shaking the pan until you can smell their aromas in the air. This will take 2–3 minutes. Remove from the heat and set aside.

When cool, tip these, along with the garlic, ginger, vinegar, tamarind paste, sugar and 125ml (½ cup) cold water into a small blender and blitz until smooth. Tip it out into a bowl and add the ground turmeric and salt to your taste – it's best not to put the turmeric into the blender or you'll turn it yellow! If not using the paste straight away, transfer to an airtight container, cover the surface with oil and store in the fridge for up to 2 weeks.

Next, prepare the pork. Line a baking tray with two long sheets of extra-wide kitchen foil, crossing them over each other. Remove the string holding the joint together and put the pork skin side down on top of the foil. Slather the paste all over the pork, pushing it into every open crevice. Wrap the pork in the foil, sealing well, and marinate in the fridge overnight.

When you're ready to cook, remove the joint from the fridge and carefully unwrap it. Toss the sliced onions in 2 tablespoons of the oil and drop them on top of the pork. Pour over the remaining oil, sprinkle on the salt and re-wrap the joint in the foil. Leave the pork to come to room temperature while you pre-heat the oven to 200°C/Fan 180°C/Gas 6.

Shove the wrapped joint in the oven and cook for 3½ hours until the pork falls apart when prodded with a fork. Unwrap the top of the foil, spoon over some of the juices and return to the oven to brown, uncovered, for another 20 minutes.

Shred the joint with two forks, mixing in the spices and oils that have oozed onto the bottom of the foil parcel. The fat will have melted into the meat. Any bits that are stuck to the foil can simply be discarded.

TIP   For a larger joint (1.8–2.2kg), simply increase the ingredients by 50 per cent and use the same cooking times.

BRUNCH

THE PHRASE 'BREAKFAST OF CHAMPIONS' MUST HAVE ORIGINATED IN INDIA.

We are a nation of savoury cooked breakfast lovers, and by cooked I don't mean beans on toast. We're talking wholesome, heaving plates of fried, steamed and sautéed goodies.

When I was growing up, weekday breakfasts were continental in style. Whatever we had for breakfast was served with a lump of fresh turmeric dipped in raw honey — for its anti-ageing properties, according to my mother's infinite wisdom. The weekends were more luxurious as we would eat this first meal of the day a little later than usual, enjoying fried flatbreads, pancakes of various descriptions and semolina steeped with sizzled curry leaves and vegetables. This chapter pays homage to those lazier mornings, more likely to feature in a weekend brunch than a quick breakfast before school or work.

The recipes here celebrate the diversity of grains and pulses used in Indian cooking. Flattened rice for instance, is probiotic, and can be turned into moreish Poha, or to help ferment south Indian crispy Dosa (crepes). Gluten-free options feature aplenty. Chilla (gram flour pancakes) and Pesarattu (whole moong crepes) are a great savoury alternative to wheat flour pancakes or omelettes. When you have weekend guests Kedgeree makes an impressive morning feast, while Egg Roast Appam can be prepared in advance for a lavish treat, guaranteed to transport you to the balmy backwaters of Kerala.

So don't settle for avo on toast in favour of a spice-filled Indian brunch. Why not invite your friends round and make a proper occasion of it?

ANDA BHURJI
MASALA SCRAMBLED EGGS WITH KALE

SERVES 4
2 tbsp oil
1 tsp cumin seeds
4 shallots, thinly sliced
4 green chillies, chopped
12 cherry tomatoes, halved
½ tsp ground turmeric
½ tsp chilli powder
2 large handfuls of kale,
    stalks removed and discarded
    and leaves chopped
8 large eggs
Salt
Toast or rotis, to serve

These scrambled eggs with cumin seeds, shallot, green chillies and tomatoes bring heady flavours to the breakfast table. They also make a delicious quick supper; any leftovers are a great filling for toasted sandwiches.

Anda Bhurji is a great way to use up leftover vegetables. I love to add handfuls of kale, which I always have in the fridge. Feel free to improvise with peppers, carrots and other vegetables chopped into little pieces. With all this inbuilt versatility, it's no wonder this dish features so regularly in Indian home kitchens.

Pour the oil into a wok and place over a high heat; when it's hot, toss in the cumin seeds. As they sizzle up, stir in the shallots and sauté for 5 minutes until pale golden.

Add half the chopped chillies to the wok with the halved tomatoes and cook for a couple of minutes until the tomatoes soften, then mix in the turmeric, chilli powder and kale.

Add salt to taste and lower the heat to medium, while you quickly crack the eggs into a bowl and give them a whisk. Pour the eggs into the wok and stir through until the eggs are well combined with the spicy mixture. Spoon onto toast or rotis, garnish with the remaining green chillies and serve.

VARIATION ➤ PANEER BHURJI
Replace the eggs with 500g crumbled or grated paneer to turn this into the perfect stuffing for Dosa (page 110) or a vegetarian version of Kati Rolls (page 155).

BESAN KA CHILLA
SAVOURY GRAM FLOUR PANCAKES

MAKES 12
300g (2½ cups) gram flour
300ml lukewarm water
¼ tsp ground turmeric
½ tsp chilli powder
½ tsp carom seeds
Salt
Oil for frying

These delicate gram flour chilla (or *cheela*), crispy at the edges and soft in the middle, are a gluten-free alternative to traditional pancakes. My grandmother used to whip these up for us when we got home from school, hangry and ready to raid the kitchen cupboards. I remember watching her deft hands in the batter, manually removing the smallest of lumps before frying the pancakes on an oil-splattered flat griddle.

As I usually make these on chaotic, family-filled mornings, I make life easy by using a blender, a medium frying pan and a ladle to get just about enough batter into the pan for perfectly shaped pancakes every time. Keep Hara Chutney (page 216) handy for dunking.

Blitz the gram flour, water, turmeric and chilli powder in a blender until smooth. Or whisk by hand; just make sure you add the water slowly to prevent lumps from forming. Stir in the carom seeds and salt to taste.

Place a frying pan over a high heat with a tablespoon or generous spray of oil. Make sure the base of the pan is coated. Lower the heat to medium and spoon a ladleful of the batter into the pan, as you would a pancake, then quickly swirl it around to make sure it covers the whole base of the pan.

Let this cook for 2 minutes until you see pores appearing and the top starts to set. The bottom of the pancake should have turned webbed and golden. Flip over and cook for another minute. Loosen the edges and lift onto a plate to serve, then get on with the next one. These are best eaten straight away but you can keep them warm by wrapping them in a tea towel lined with foil.

VARIATIONS

> VEGETABLE CHILLA
Top the setting pancake with a combination of thinly sliced red onions, grated courgette, chopped spinach or quartered cherry tomatoes to turn this into a more substantial meal.

> PUDLA
Gujaratis do a lovely version of this with grated ginger, chopped green chillies and fresh coriander. Just leave the carom seeds out.

UPMA
SPICE-TEMPERED VEGETABLE SEMOLINA

SERVES 4–6
300g (2 cups) coarse semolina
2 tbsp oil
¼ tsp asafoetida
2 tsp mustard seeds
Handful of curry leaves
2 tsp skinless black gram lentils
2 whole dried red chillies
1 medium onion, finely chopped
2 medium carrots, diced
5 green beans
Handful of peas
2 green chillies, chopped
1 tbsp chopped coriander
1 tbsp ghee
1.25 litres (5 cups) hot water
Salt

Upma is a typical south Indian brunch dish that also hits the spot as a light lunch or teatime snack. Its creamy yet grainy texture has a moreish, melt-in-the-mouth quality. Roasting the coarse semolina first before cooking it is essential for good upma.

The first time I made this I took the non-stick coating off my frying pan with a bit of overzealous elbow action, so go easy on the scraping when you toast the semolina. For ease you can replace the vegetables suggested here with 2 cups of frozen chopped vegetables.

Place a robust sauté pan or heavy-based wok over a medium heat. When warm, add the semolina, stirring it gently for 5 minutes until it is evenly toasted.

Tip the semolina out of the pan into a bowl. Rinse the pan, wipe it dry and add the oil, then put it back over a high heat. When hot, tip in the asafoetida, then throw in the mustard seeds, curry leaves, skinless black gram lentils and whole dried red chillies. As they start sizzling, stir in the onion. Fry for about 2 minutes until the onion softens.

Add the vegetables and green chillies and stir with a few tablespoons of water until the vegetables are tender. Season generously with salt, to allow for the semolina that's about to enter the scene.

Tip the semolina back into the pan, followed by the chopped coriander, ghee and hot water. Stir the whole lot vigorously until there are no dry bits of semolina left and it doubles in volume. It should be moist and grainy in texture; there will be lumps, but this is totally normal. You can either serve the upma in individual bowls or pour it into a large shallow bowl, allow it to set and then tip it out and slice it like a cake. You can serve this hot, but it's just as nice at room temperature.

TIP   If you have it handy, replace the coarse semolina with 260g (2 cups) fine semolina for a creamier, smoother upma.

RAVA UTTAPAM
GINGERED SEMOLINA PANCAKES

MAKES 8

FOR THE PANCAKES
130g (1 cup) fine semolina
4 tbsp Greek-style yoghurt
2 tbsp rice flour
1cm fresh root ginger, finely grated
½ tsp salt
375ml (1½ cups) lukewarm water
¼ tsp bicarbonate of soda
Coconut oil for frying

FOR THE TOPPINGS (OPTIONAL)
Chopped coriander
Thinly sliced peppers
Thinly sliced shallots
Halved cherry tomatoes

Uttapam is one of south India's breakfast delights. The pancakes are traditionally made with a fermented batter, which means these soft pancakes can be enjoyed in vast quantities but still digested easily. My recipe is more of an 'instant' version, which needs minimal prep and time investment.

While a plain Uttapam is lovely dunked into the coconut chutney on page 218, you can crown yours with a liberal handful of any of the toppings suggested below. Make the pancakes in a small frying pan for the perfect shape every time. Uttapam can be prepared the night before and stored in an airtight container, then reheated in a microwave until warm.

Put the semolina, yoghurt, rice flour, ginger and salt into a medium bowl. Now, add the water a little at a time, mixing into a thick dough to remove any lumps, then whisking to a smooth batter.

Mix the bicarbonate of soda into the batter and then leave to sit for 10 minutes while you get your toppings ready. Place a small frying pan over a high heat. When the pan is hot, lower the heat to medium and dot a bit of coconut oil on. The pan should be greasy to prevent sticking but not flooded with oil, so use a piece of kitchen paper to wipe the oil over the surface.

Pour a ladleful of batter into the pan. Wait for 2 minutes until the surface starts sporting little holes and the edges solidify. Generously sprinkle the setting surface with your choice of topping, if using. Flip over and cook for another 2 minutes.

Dot a little coconut oil around the edges of the pancake, flip over once more and cook for a few more seconds. Remove from the pan and then start cooking the next one. Serve hot.

KANDA POHA

LEMONY FLATTENED RICE AND ONION PULAO

SERVES 4

400g (4 cups) thick flattened rice
2 tbsp oil
½ tsp asafoetida
2 tsp mustard seeds
20 curry leaves
2 tsp raw skinless peanuts
1 large onion, finely chopped
2 green chillies, finely chopped
2 tsp ground turmeric
4 tsp lemon juice
Salt

TO SERVE

4 lemon wedges
2 tbsp chopped coriander
Shredded fresh coconut (optional)
Fried gram flour noodles (optional)

This breakfast staple from the state of Maharashtra combines lemon-drenched 'flattened' rice with a tempering of onions, curry leaves and mustard seeds. *Kanda* means 'onions' in Marathi, and *poha* (also sold as *pawa*) is rice that is partially cooked, beaten and then dried, during which time it ferments and transforms into a flat, airy and soft version of itself – flattened rice.

The trick with flattened rice is to wash it with cold water to fluff up the grains, without letting it get soggy. Traditionally, Kanda Poha is served topped with freshly scraped coconut and fried gram flour noodles, or sev (page 238).

In a large mixing bowl, wash the flattened rice well and then drain and leave to sit for 10 minutes to allow it to slowly swell up.

Pour the oil into a wok and place over a medium-high heat. When it's hot, drop in the asafoetida, mustard seeds, curry leaves and peanuts. As soon as they sizzle, stir through the onion and green chillies. Sauté for a couple of minutes until the onion softens.

Add the turmeric, stirring to coat the onion evenly, then stir in the flattened rice, a little at a time, taking care not to break up the grains. Tip in any water remaining in the bowl the rice was sitting in, increase the heat to a high simmer, cover and cook for a couple of minutes.

To finish, pour the lemon juice all over and add salt to taste. Give the rice a final stir. Serve with lemon wedges, coriander and, if using, the shredded coconut and fried gram flour noodles.

VARIATIONS

> BATATA POHA
Add a large handful of peeled and diced potato to the wok with the onions and chillies and sauté until cooked, then proceed as above.

> CHIRWE KA PULAO
Add 2 chopped tomatoes and 2 handfuls of chopped veg (carrots, beans, cauliflower) when the onions are soft. Add 2 tablespoons of hot water and cook until the additional vegetables are soft before proceeding as above.

PESARATTU
GINGER AND CHILLI MOONG BEAN CREPES

MAKES 12
200g (1 cup) whole green moong beans
2.5cm fresh root ginger, finely grated
2 green chillies, finely chopped
2 tbsp chopped coriander
Salt
Oil for frying

FOR THE TOPPINGS
Coconut Chutney (page 218)
Sliced green chillies
Sliced red onions

These crisp crepes from the state of Andhra Pradesh, made with whole green moong beans, are bursting with fresh and earthy ginger, coriander and chilli. Consider this recipe as a gentle introduction to making Dosa (page 110); it uses a similar technique but requires no overnight soaking or fermenting. You will need a high-speed blender to make smooth crepe batter and a non-stick or well-seasoned pancake pan.

If the swirl technique described below isn't for you, just use a ladle and a small frying pan to get perfectly round pancakes every time. Traditionally, you would serve these with Coconut Chutney (page 218), sliced green chillies and raw onions.

Wash the moong beans by rinsing in a sieve under a cold tap until the water runs clear. Tip into a glass or non-metallic bowl, add plenty of cold water and leave to soak for 2 hours.

When the time is up and they have swollen to almost twice their size, drain and place in a blender with 375ml (1½ cups) cold water, the ginger and green chillies and blend until you get a smooth batter. Now stir in the chopped coriander and salt to your taste. The batter keeps for a day without losing colour and thickens in texture so you will need to loosen it with a bit of cold water to get a pancake consistency if you make this in advance.

Place a crepe or pancake pan over a high heat with a teaspoon of oil. The pan needs to be greasy to avoid sticking but not too oily – as the oil heats in the pan, use a spatula to spread the oil around the base of the pan, wiping off any excess gently with kitchen paper. When the pan is hot, lower the heat to medium, giving the pan a few seconds to adjust to the new temperature. If all this sounds complicated, it really isn't. As with everything, practice makes perfect.

Now, spoon a ladleful of batter into the centre of the pan and quickly use the base of the ladle to swirl the batter around the pan in a giant circle. You will get webbed areas in the crepe, which is a good thing as it makes it crisp.

   ∨   Recipe continues on page 102

Leave the crepe to cook for 2 minutes, drizzling a teaspoon of oil over the surface of the crepe and tilting or shaking the pan to spread this around. The base of the crepe should be golden and crisp; you can sneakily peek by lifting an edge to check. When it's done, slide the crepe out of the pan and onto a plate. Keep warm while you make the rest of the crepes.

TIP   My friend Arundati, who made these for me in Hyderabad, recommends adding a couple of tablespoons of rice flour to the batter to make them crispy. However, Aunty, who makes the most incredible ones in her famous restaurant in Vishakhapatnam, doesn't. Over to you.

EGG ROAST APPAM
KERALAN EGG MASALA ON COCONUT PANCAKES

SERVES 4–6

FOR THE PANCAKES
180g rice (regular or basmati),
    plus 4 tbsp
1 × 400ml tin coconut milk
    (at least 75% coconut)
2 tsp sugar
1 tsp fast-action dried yeast
Salt
Oil for frying

FOR THE EGG MASALA
8 medium eggs
8 tbsp coconut oil
1 tsp mustard seeds
2 medium onions (about 250g),
    halved and sliced
4 small green chillies, chopped
20 curry leaves
8 garlic cloves, finely grated
5cm fresh root ginger, finely grated
8 medium ripe tomatoes, diced
1 tsp ground turmeric
4 tsp ground coriander
1 tbsp Kashmiri chilli powder or paprika
½ tsp freshly ground black pepper
Salt
Coriander leaves, to garnish (optional)

This is a Keralan breakfast guaranteed to set your taste buds up for the day. Crispy at the edges and spongy in the middle, coconut milk pancakes (*appam*) are served with eggs coated in a fragrant masala. Here the Hindi interpretation of roast means that the eggs are 'cooked whole' but in other dishes it can also mean 'cooked without the addition of water'.

I have watched the chefs at Coconut Lagoon in Kerala's Kumarakom in amazement as they used a seasoned cast-iron dish called an *appa chatti* and a very fine wooden spatula to delicately prise the pancakes off their edges. A toothpick is also sometimes used by experts to dislodge the pancake without ripping it. For the rest of us, the two simple methods below make a breeze of this – just bear in mind that you'll need to factor in the time needed for soaking and resting.

First get your pancakes going. Wash and soak the 180g rice in 1.1 litres (4½ cups) cold water for 3–4 hours. Meanwhile, bubble the remaining 4 tablespoons of rice and 8 tablespoons of hot water in a pan for 8–10 minutes, or until cooked. Leave to sit without draining. Cooked rice partially ferments, and this fermentation will enhance the taste and texture of your pancakes.

When the soaking time is up, drain and blend the uncooked rice with the coconut milk, the cooked rice and its water, the sugar and yeast. Add salt to your taste. Pour this appam batter into a bowl and shove it in a warm place to rest for another 3–4 hours, or overnight. The oven with its light on but no heat will suffice.

Next make a start on the egg masala. Place the eggs in a pan of cold water, bring to the boil and cook for 8–10 minutes. Drain and rinse in cold water; when cool enough to handle, peel and set aside.

Put the coconut oil in a sauté pan or wok and place over a medium-high heat. When it's hot, toss in the mustard seeds and, as they sizzle up, stir in the onions and a pinch of salt. Stir for 5 minutes until the onions start to colour.

Recipe continues on page 105

Next, toss in the green chillies, curry leaves, garlic and ginger. Cook this for another 10–12 minutes until the onions are golden, then add the tomatoes and stir through for a couple of minutes until soft.

Now, add the turmeric, coriander, chilli powder or paprika and pepper. Mix through and cook for 5 minutes until the tomatoes turn pulpy and the raw smell of the spices disappears. Lower the heat to a high simmer and cook for 10 minutes, covered, until you see oil oozing through the masala and it turns a deeper shade of red. You'll need to keep an eye on it and keep stirring from time to time. If it gets stuck to the bottom of the pan, add a dash of hot water and scrape it off. Taste and add salt. Finish the egg masala by making shallow slits in the hard-boiled eggs and stirring them through the masala. (You can also prepare the egg masala the night before and just warm it up in a wok while you're making the appam.)

Check that your batter still has a pancake-like dropping consistency, as you need to be able to swirl it in the pan to achieve the cloud-like soft middles and thin, crisp edges. Add a tablespoon or two of water to loosen if not.

There are two ways to make the pancakes. The traditional way is to warm a small lightly oiled non-stick wok over a medium heat. Take a ladleful of batter and pour it into the middle, then quickly swirl the wok around to get a thin layer around the sides. Cover and cook for 2–3 minutes until the middle is set and the edges curl up and are crisp and golden. Prise the edges free with a wooden bamboo skewer – it should dislodge easily – then tip out and keep warm while you repeat to make more pancakes.

The non-traditional way, and the one I use most often (with apologies to every native Keralan), is to cook these on a flat griddle. The edges separate and fold upwards when done. The only thing you have to do is make sure the batter is thicker in the middle to get the characteristic spongy centre.

Serve the pancakes with the egg masala inside, garnished with coriander leaves, if liked. Serve any extra pancakes on the side.

ALOO PARATHAS
PUNJABI POTATO FLATBREADS

MAKES 8
300g floury potatoes
Juice of ½ lemon
1 tbsp finely chopped coriander
1 large green chilli, finely chopped
1 tsp salt
120g (1 cup) chappati flour, plus extra
    for rolling
1 tbsp oil, plus extra for shallow-frying
1–2 tbsp yoghurt
Butter

A staple Punjabi breakfast, these legendary flatbreads are stuffed with potatoes and then shallow-fried and served — in an ideal world — with lashings of white butter churned from thick cream. They are stacked one on top of another, and are usually enjoyed with a chilled glass of lassi or some natural yoghurt. My grandmother was an expert at making these the traditional way, where the dough pocket is filled, then rolled out carefully and shallow-fried.

Of course, this is far too much effort for me so I've used a non-stuff method. Before I got half decent at rolling, I used a large round cookie cutter to punch out perfect shapes — do the same if aesthetics are your thing. Keep butter handy — it would be rude not to stick a lump on each paratha as it comes off the griddle.

Boil the potatoes in a large pan of salted water until soft. Drain and when cool enough to handle, peel and place in a bowl. Squeeze in the lemon juice and tip in the coriander, green chilli and salt. Mash the potato well, mixing until the ingredients are well combined.

Now, add half the chappati flour and the tablespoon of oil and mix well with the potatoes, using your hands. Add a tablespoon of the yoghurt and then the rest of the flour. Mix again, kneading to get soft pliable dough. Punch and roll backwards and forwards for a good 5 minutes.

Add the other tablespoon of yoghurt if you need it to soften the dough and incorporate all the flour. Cover the ball of dough with a damp tea towel or muslin and fire up a flat griddle over a medium heat. Measure the dough out into eight equal portions — you can use an ice cream scoop to do this, or just roll out a fat sausage and cut it into eight equal parts. Place them back in the bowl and cover.

Get out a chopping board. Put 3 tablespoons of flour into a shallow bowl. Keep a bowl of oil and a pastry brush handy, or even better fill a salad oil drizzler with some oil. Now take the first ball and massage it in your palms until there are no cracks on its surface.

∨   Recipe continues on page 109

Now, flatten it and dip in the flour on both sides. Next, place on the board and use a rolling pin to roll it out into a circle of an even 2mm thickness. If it tears, just patch it up with your fingers – my favourite thing about these parathas are the crispy bits where the dough has split! If the dough starts sticking, sprinkle with a bit more flour.

Dust the excess flour off the paratha by placing it in the palm of one hand and then the other, shaking gently. Then place on the hot griddle for 1 minute. Flip over and cook for another minute, brushing or sprinkling a teaspoon of oil around the edges. Now turn over again for a few seconds until you see golden spots and bubbles appearing on both sides and the paratha is cooked through (this will only take a couple of minutes).

Place the paratha on a plate, dot with butter and crack on with the next one. The really experienced roll out one paratha while the other is cooking. No pressure! Serve these hot. If eating later, place the parathas on a tea towel lined with foil and wrap well to keep warm. They are excellent as picnic food eaten cold too.

DOSA
FERMENTED RICE AND LENTIL CREPES

SERVES 4–6

50g (½ cup) thick flattened rice
175g (1 cup) rice (regular or basmati)
90g (½ cup) skinless black gram lentils
25g (2 tbsp) split Bengal gram or split
    pigeon peas (optional)
1 tsp fenugreek seeds (optional)
2 tsp salt
Oil or ghee, as needed

Loved the world over, these crispy crepes are a south Indian breakfast special. They get their unique taste from a fermented lentil and parboiled rice batter, which is then swirled on a lightly greased flat griddle into a thin web. I grew up on regular trips to south Indian restaurants where the star attraction would be a peek at the chefs in action through smudgy glass, a tradition that my children are happily keeping alive. Without a doubt, dosa-making runs through the veins of every south Indian cook.

The art of making dosa boils down to the texture of the batter and the heat of the pan. My version uses flattened rice, uncooked rice, a high-speed blender and a quick overnight ferment to give you an exotic healthy breakfast that is perfect with Coconut Chutney (page 218) and Hara Chutney (page 216). Dosa batter will happily store in an airtight container for up to a week in the fridge, so you can make it well in advance.

Place the flattened rice in a sieve and wash under a cold tap. Leave to sit in the sieve for 2–3 minutes.

Wash the uncooked rice thoroughly and put into a large ceramic, glass or stainless steel bowl. Add the flattened rice to the bowl, then rinse and add in both types of lentils. The job of the Bengal gram or split pigeon peas is to add a lovely golden colour to the dosa, but you can leave them out if you don't have them. Add 750ml (3 cups) cold water and leave to soak for 3–4 hours.

When the soaking time is up, drain the rice and lentils and then add to a blender with the fenugreek seeds, if using, and 375ml (1½ cups) cold water. Blend into a thick, smooth batter – a high-speed blender or smoothie maker works best. Pour the batter back into the bowl.

Pre-heat the oven to its lowest setting (120°C/Fan 100°C/Gas ½), then switch the heat off but leave the light on to maintain a steady warmth. Loosely cover the bowl with a damp tea towel or muslin and leave in the oven overnight or for at least 10 hours. Traditionally, dosa is made after two days of fermenting, but that's just a little bit too long to keep the oven occupied and with its light going!

Recipe continues on page 112

When the time is up, you will have a frothy batter of pouring consistency. Stir the salt through. Place a non-stick flat griddle over a high heat and get a spatula and a soup ladle ready. Lightly grease the griddle and wipe off any excess oil with kitchen paper.

When the griddle is hot, lower the heat to medium. You want it hot enough for the dosa to turn golden crisp, but cool enough to be able to swirl it without the batter turning lumpy. Drops of water should sizzle when they land on the griddle, but if it's smoking it's too hot.

Now, pour a ladleful of the batter into the centre of the griddle and using the base of the ladle, swirl it in a circular spiral motion to spread the batter into a circle about 15cm in diameter. Drizzle or brush the top of the dosa with a little oil or ghee and leave for 2 minutes to cook.

To see if the dosa is done, you can prise one edge up to check for a caramel-coloured underside. If it's pale, keep going. When you get a golden base, fold one edge over the rest of the dosa, lift out with the spatula and transfer to a plate.

Continue until all the batter is used up. Usual pancake rules apply – the first one or two will be rubbish but you'll be amazed at the ones that follow.

VARIATIONS ❯ PAPER DOSA
When you get into the swing of things, you can scrape some of the fluffy batter off the top of the dosa to thin it out and then flip it over. The dosa will be paper-thin and crispy and can be rolled up in a tube to serve.

❯ PANEER DOSA
Place a tablespoon of Paneer Bharta (page 143) or Paneer Bhurji (page 92) in the centre of the dosa before you fold over and serve.

ANDA PARATHAS
GLUTEN-FREE EGGY FLATBREADS

MAKES 4

200ml whole milk

4 large eggs

18 tbsp gluten-free plain flour

1 small onion, finely chopped

1 small green chilli, finely chopped

1 tsp salt

4 tsp oil

TO SERVE

1 small onion, sliced and drizzled
   with lemon juice

Coriander leaves

Ketchup

This all-in-one breakfast meal is like an omelette spiked with green chillies and onions crossed with a paratha. In India, this was a regular feature in our home, where we would make an omelette and add a paratha to the not-quite-set surface before flipping it over to finish cooking.

Now, I make these parathas as a thick, eggy pancake with gluten-free flour, mixing up the batter for each pancake as I go. They make a filling yet very easily digestible way to start the day.

Pour 50ml of the milk into a measuring jug then crack an egg into it. Whisk them together, then add 4½ tablespoons of the gluten-free flour to the jug and mix together well, whisking to remove any lumps. Take a quarter of the onion and green chilli and stir through, along with ¼ teaspoon of salt.

Put a teaspoon of the oil into a small frying pan and place over a medium heat, swirling to coat the base of the pan. Then pour the batter into the frying pan in a circular motion, starting with the edges first. Swirl the batter round to make sure you get thick edges or you'll get more of a pancake than paratha effect (this only really matters for the finicky among you).

Give the paratha a couple of minutes for the surface to seal, then flip over and cook, pressing down hard with a spatula to make sure no bits are left uncooked. When this side starts showing golden spots and the paratha is firm, lift it onto a plate and start again with the next one.

Top the parathas with lemon-drizzled sliced onions and coriander leaves and serve hot, with ketchup.

TIP   If you're not too fussed about even-sized parathas, you could simply mix the batter all in one go and attempt to portion it up evenly.

KEDGEREE
BUTTERED RICE WITH HADDOCK AND PEAS

SERVES 4

350g basmati rice

4 smoked haddock fillets
    (about 500g), fresh or frozen

400ml whole milk

4 eggs

75g butter or ghee

1 large onion, finely chopped

1 tsp ground coriander

1 tsp ground cumin

½ tsp ground turmeric

200g (1 heaped cup) frozen peas

Salt and freshly ground black pepper

Handful of parsley or coriander leaves

Lemon halves, to serve

This Anglo-Indian buttered rice and peas with flaked haddock is a throwback to the days of the British Raj. Introduced to the widely eaten rice and lentil *khichdi*, the British embraced it for breakfast, incorporating their beloved smoked fish into it and eventually doing away with the lentils entirely.

Kedgeree is my go-to brunch crowd-pleaser, as I almost always have bags of frozen smoked haddock fillets at home. It's easy to cook this in giant quantities and serve on a large platter that the whole family and visiting relatives and friends can tuck into. Whizz up some cold lassi (page 189) and crack out your pickle collection to do this dish full justice.

First cook the rice according to the packet instructions or by following my method for perfect basmati (page 162).

Place the haddock fillets in a sauté pan, pour over the milk and bring to the boil. When it starts bubbling, lower to a simmer and poach the haddock fillets until the flesh flakes easily – this will take about 8 minutes for fresh fish and 10 minutes for frozen. Drain and set aside, reserving the milk.

Meanwhile, boil the eggs to your liking – 6 minutes for soft-boiled or 8–10 minutes for hard-boiled. We often go for hard-boiled eggs because of fussy little terrors in the family, but runny-yolked ones are nicer if you ask me. Drench the boiled eggs in cold water, then peel and set aside.

Put the butter or ghee into a large wok and place over a high heat. When it's hot, toss in the onion and sauté for 5 minutes. Add the ground spices and frozen peas and sauté for another minute. Then stir in the rice with half the reserved milk, mixing well until the rice is coated with the onion mixture. Gently fold the haddock in, letting it flake but not crumble.

Stir in salt and pepper to taste and spoon onto a platter or into bowls. Halve or quarter the peeled eggs and place on top of the rice. Serve sprinkled with parsley or coriander and lemon halves on the side.

SMALL
BITES

IN INDIA, SNACKS ARE A BONA FIDE MEALTIME MOMENT.

They feature whenever hunger strikes: at elevenses, in the middle of the afternoon, typically with a cup of chai in tow, or as nibbles with evening drinks.

When I was little, teatime treats were a must when we got home, ravenous from long days at school followed by extracurricular activities. By evening my mother's seventies-style *hors d'oeuvres* would appear on a glass trolley to accompany the two drinks my grandfather enjoyed before dinner. But these little morsels were not just for the home; they were often packed up for long car journeys and picnics in the great outdoors.

This chapter includes savoury nibbles for every occasion, with a quick and easy twist on many of them. As I would rather not have to watch a wok full of sizzling oil and then subsequently smell of it for the rest of the day, the oven frequently steps in to assist. So oven-baked pakoras and bhajis are crispy things that go perfectly with a warming cup of Adrakwali Chai (page 192) on rainy days. Masala Badam is great for the munchies, while trays of Masala Vada and Dhokla are effortless snacks to take, smug-faced, to potluck gatherings.

While the concept of a starter that you sit down to eat before a main course doesn't really apply in Indian food, Machli ke Cutlets and Samosas work well as nibbles with drinks ahead of dinner, accompanied by chutneys for dipping, dunking and slathering.

So say goodbye to those mid-afternoon energy slumps and pre-dinner hunger pangs with the punchy and practical snacks in the pages that follow.

PYAAJ PAKORA
BAKED BATTERED ONIONS

MAKES 10–12
Oil spray
8 tbsp gram flour
4 tbsp rice flour
½ tsp salt
½ tsp ground turmeric
½ tsp carom seeds
½ tsp ground coriander
½ tsp chilli powder
2 small onions (250g), sliced

Crispy on the outside, soft on the inside and providing a spice explosion in your mouth, onion pakoras are irresistible in every way. While they are often confused with bhajis, which have a spongy batter that takes centre stage, they are quite different. With pakoras, the batter plays second fiddle and the vegetable is the star, much like Japanese tempura.

As I don't deep-fry at home I have grown a few grey hairs trialling the perfect oven-friendly recipe. The secret is rice flour to help the pakoras stay crisp. To get crispy onion strands that sing, don't slice them too thinly. I don't want to go all pedantic on you but the perfect size is about 4mm wide. Try serving these with Nimbu Ka Achar (page 223).

Pre-heat the oven to 200°C/Fan 180°C/Gas 6. Line a couple of baking sheets with baking parchment and spray 10–12 evenly spaced spots with oil.

Sift the gram flour and rice flour into a mixing bowl (sifting will help create a lump-free batter). Now, add the salt, turmeric, carom seeds, ground coriander and chilli powder. Add 6 tablespoons of cold water and mix well, turning the spiced flours into a thick paste and squashing any lumps that may form.

Add the onions to the batter and stir them through for a couple of minutes to completely coat them with the batter. They will soften slightly too, as they release moisture when stirred.

Now, using a couple of tablespoons, load even amounts of batter-covered onions onto the spots of oil on the baking sheets. Bring any stray bits of onion close to the mound so you don't get too many burnt edges – a few are no bad thing as they'll add to the crispiness of the end result.

When the onions are all used up, spray each mound with more oil and shove in the oven for 20 minutes. Remove from the oven, flip the pakoras over and cook for another 10 minutes. Allow to rest for 5 minutes before you tuck in.

Pictured with Sabzi Bhaji (page 120), Masala Chai (page 192) and Nimbu Ka Achar (page 223).   119

SABZI BHAJI
KALE AND COURGETTE FRITTERS

MAKES 8–10
Oil spray
2 handfuls of kale or spinach
4 green chillies, finely chopped
60g (½ cup) gram flour
¾ tsp salt
1 tsp carom seeds
1 tsp ground turmeric
½ tsp bicarbonate of soda
100g courgette
175g sweet potato, peeled

These soft, spicy bites with courgette and kale are so simple to put together. They also double up as an excellent base for a poached egg, as I discovered on a visit to Edinburgh. Scotland houses the largest concentration of serious bhaji lovers outside of India, by my calculations.

The word *bhaji* can cause all sorts of confusion – it can mean fried, sautéed or a curry. To most people, though, it means deep-fried, gram flour-battered vegetables. Importantly a bhaji is different to a pakora, which has a much lighter texture. This recipe is my humble ode to the bhajis so loved in Britain, except that they are light, fresh and baked!

Pre-heat the oven to 200°C/Fan 180°C/Gas 6. Line a baking sheet with baking parchment and spray 8–10 evenly spaced spots with oil.

If using kale, remove the tough stalks and roughly chop the leaves. Put the kale or spinach into a large bowl along with the green chillies, gram flour, salt, carom seeds, turmeric and bicarbonate of soda. Grate the courgette and sweet potato – I often use my food processor for this – and tip into the bowl too.

Now mix the whole lot together with your hands, squeezing to extract the moisture from the vegetables and allowing it to combine with the flour to act as a binding agent. If you need more moisture, add a couple of tablespoons of cold water.

Then, using a tablespoon, drop equal quantities of the batter onto the oil spots on the lined baking sheet. Spray with a little oil and bake for 25 minutes.

Let the bhajis cool slightly before you dive into them. Like pakoras, they are lovely with green Hara Chutney (page 216) or one of my Instachutneys (page 219).

RAJMA GALOUTI KEBAB
KIDNEY BEAN AND SWEET POTATO CAKES

MAKES 4–6

2 small or 1 large sweet
  potato (350g)
1 × 400g tin kidney beans, rinsed
  and drained
1cm fresh root ginger, finely grated
2 garlic cloves, finely grated
1 tsp ground cumin
½ tsp chilli powder
1 tbsp cornflour
3 tbsp oil or ghee
Salt

Devilishly simple to make, these melt-in-the-mouth earthy bites put a tin of kidney beans and a sweet potato to excellent use. *Galouti* means 'melting', and we have the food-loving, cross-dressing Mughal emperor Wajid Ali Shah to thank for this kebab. He eventually lost his teeth but not his voracious appetite, inspiring this kebab, which barely needs chewing! The original galouti is meat-based of course, but I am sure he would have approved of my vegan version.

Bake the sweet potato in its skin to preserve the goodness. For a more decadent Mughlai feel, use ghee, if you have it. Serve with a leafy green salad and your favourite chutney.

Prick the sweet potatoes with a fork and bake them in their skins. I do this in a 1000W microwave and it takes about 8–10 minutes. Alternatively, bake directly on the shelf of an oven pre-heated to 220°C/Fan 200°C/Gas 7 for 45 minutes.

Meanwhile, toss the drained kidney beans into a bowl with the ginger and garlic.

When the potatoes are soft, carefully peel off their skins and add the fleshy part to the kidney beans. Now add the ground cumin, chilli powder, cornflour and salt to taste and mash the whole lot together. Chill for 20 minutes.

When the time is up, pre-heat the grill to high. Line a baking sheet with baking parchment and spread the oil or ghee all over it. Then with a deep spoon or spring-loaded ice cream scoop, take a ball of the dough and fashion it into a little cake. Place it on the oiled parchment and then flip it over so both sides are greased. Continue until all the mixture is used up. The size of the kebabs is entirely up to you and depends on how substantial you want each one to be.

Place the tray under the grill and cook for 12–15 minutes until the tops are golden and crispy. Remove the tray and leave to cool for 5 minutes before sliding the kebabs off the parchment and serving them hot.

MASALA VADA
BENGAL GRAM AND CURRY LEAF CAKES

MAKES 10–12
190g (1 cup) split Bengal gram
2.5cm fresh root ginger, roughly
   chopped
1 medium onion, finely chopped
Small handful of coriander leaves,
   finely chopped
15 curry leaves, roughly chopped
2–3 green chillies, finely chopped
2 tbsp rice flour
1 tsp salt
4 tbsp oil

An addictive teatime snack, vada feature as street food throughout south India. The word *vada* is pronounced with a rolling 'r' (*vur-ha*), and refers to any savoury fried cake or veggie burger.

Normally vada are deep-fried but I bake them – a thinner shape will give you a crisper end result. Dunk these in chutney if you wish, but they are so good on their own that you can happily enjoy them just the way they are.

Rinse the lentils in a sieve until the water runs clear, then soak them in a non-metallic bowl with 500ml (2 cups) cold water for 4 hours.

When the time is up, pre-heat the oven to 200°C/Fan 180°C/Gas 6 and line a baking sheet with foil or baking parchment.

Drain the lentils and put into a blender or food processor, reserving a handful in the bowl. Add the ginger and then blitz until you get a coarse paste that comes together in the blender.

Now, tip the lentil batter back into the bowl with the whole lentils. Add the chopped onion, coriander, curry leaves, green chillies, rice flour and salt. Mix everything together well.

Rub half the oil over the lined baking sheet. Shove the sheet into the oven for a minute to warm up, then take it out. Now just scoop the fritters directly onto the sheet with an ice cream scoop and gently flatten the tops. You roughly want a flying saucer shape. Piece any bits back together if they fall apart.

When all the batter is used up, bake for 15 minutes, then remove from the oven, flip over and drizzle with the remaining oil. Return to the oven for another 15 minutes until golden and crispy. The vadas are lovely fresh out of the oven, but are equally moreish cold.

SAFED DHOKLA
FERMENTED RICE AND LENTIL CAKE

MAKES 16
90g (½ cup) skinless black gram lentils
45g (¼ cup) rice (regular or basmati)
1cm fresh root ginger, finely grated
½ green chilli, finely chopped
1 tsp salt
¼ tsp bicarbonate of soda
Oil for greasing
2 pinches of chilli powder
2 pinches of ground cumin
2 pinches of coarsely ground
    black pepper
Finely chopped coriander, to serve

Safed (or white dhokla) is a spongy rice and lentil cake from the state of Gujarat, a predominantly vegetarian state that boasts a great heritage in savoury snacks. This recipe for a fermented version came from our Gujarati adopted-granny-of-sorts. Traditionally, an over-the-counter antacid called ENO is used as the raising agent but bicarbonate of soda does the job just as well.

My experiments with the perfect spot for fermenting in cold, grey climes included the airing cupboard, the boiler room and the electric cable shelf. But the best place is overnight in an oven with the light on but no heat. Come the morning, you'll have the frothy, heaving bowl of goodness you need. Make sure you allow for 4 hours of soaking before you can start fermenting.

Put the lentils and rice into a sieve and wash thoroughly under the tap until the water runs clear. Tip into a large glass or non-metallic bowl, add 375ml (1½ cups) cold water and leave to soak for at least 4 hours, or overnight if you prefer.

When the time is up, drain the rice and lentils and put into a blender with 125ml (½ cup) cold water. Blitz the rice and lentils into a thick batter. Pour this back into the bowl, placing it in an oven with just the light on, loosely covered with a damp tea towel. Leave this untouched for 8–10 hours. If I'm cooking the dhokla for breakfast, I leave the batter overnight but if it's for the evening, it means the oven is out of action all day. Unless it's a warm day, in which case the batter can sit on the worktop instead.

When the fermentation time is up, you'll see that the batter has risen and turned frothy. Add the ginger, chilli, salt and bicarbonate of soda and stir through just a couple of times.

Pre-heat the oven to 200°C/Fan 180°C/Gas 6 and lightly oil the base and sides of a 20–23cm brownie tin.

Recipe continues on page 126

Pour the batter into the tin, smoothing over the top with a spatula, and sprinkle the chilli powder, ground cumin and black pepper over the top. Loosely cover with foil or baking parchment, place on a baking sheet and slide into the hot oven for 15 minutes, or until a skewer comes out clean when inserted into the middle.

Take the tin out of the oven and leave the cake to cool for 5 minutes before you gently tip it out onto the baking sheet and then turn it over onto a platter, so the spices are facing up – it's a bit like turning out a cake really.

Cut the dhokla into squares and serve scattered with chopped coriander as soon as it's cool enough to handle. It is also lovely cold and dunked in Hara Chutney (page 216).

TIP   If you double the quantities and bake in a 23cm round tin for 20–25 minutes, you can slice the dhokla in wedges like a cake and feed a larger group.

MASALA BADAM
CUMIN AND TURMERIC SPICED NUTS

SERVES 2–4

2 tbsp coconut oil

400g mixed nuts (4 large handfuls)

1 tsp ground turmeric

1 tsp chilli powder

1 tsp freshly ground black pepper

1 tsp ground cumin

1½ tsp salt

In India, you can buy all sorts of bagged crunchy snacks – Bombay mix is just one of several addictive varieties featuring sev (crispy gram flour noodles), flattened rice, puffed rice and more. For this recipe, just grab a few bags of raw mixed nuts –almonds, cashews and pistachios are good choices. Tossing them in spices gives them an edge and makes for a far more exotic snack. They also make delightful gifts, tied up with gold ribbon in little bags.

Warm the oil in a wok over a medium-high heat. When it's hot, tip in the nuts and then sprinkle all the spices on top. Stir well for 2–3 minutes until the spices are sizzling, then take the wok off the heat and sprinkle over the salt.

Leave the nuts to cool down, giving the wok a good shake a couple of times to get the spicy mixture to coat them evenly. You can eat the nuts as soon as they're cool enough, or store in an airtight container for up to a week.

SAMOSAS

30-MINUTE BAKED-NOT-FRIED SAMOSAS

MAKES 12

MAKES 12
3 tbsp oil
1 tbsp ground cumin
1 tbsp ground coriander
1 tsp chilli powder
1 tsp salt
2 pinches of asafoetida
300g boiled potatoes, peeled and
    cut into large cubes
250g (½ block) ready-made
    shortcrust pastry

Crispy, crunchy and packed with flavour, this cheat's version of a samosa is guaranteed to impress. Samosas are rarely made at home; instead they are usually sourced from your preferred sweet shop. They are made using pastry that is kneaded with oil, much like roti dough, and then stuffed with spicy potato before being deep-fried. The filo pastry ones that are so common in the West are what we would call 'cocktail samosas'.

The reason that this recipe is so easy to make at home is that it uses ready-made pastry and the oven instead of a deep fryer. Make a batch for your friends and enjoy them fresh out of the oven, dipped in a sweet and spicy chutney like my Tamarind and Peanut Instachutney (page 219).

Line a baking tray with foil or baking parchment.

Pour 1½ tablespoons of the oil into a small wok or frying pan and place over a medium-high heat. While it's heating up, mix the ground cumin, ground coriander, chilli powder and salt with 2 tablespoons of lukewarm water. This will stop the spices from burning when they touch the hot oil.

When the oil is hot, add the asafoetida – this will add a touch of onion-garlic flavour to the samosa filling. Then quickly pour in the spice paste. It will sizzle up; as it does, toss in the cooked potatoes. Now break them up with a wooden spoon, to make sure there are no big lumps, as these would split the samosas. The potato filling needs to have some texture, however, so don't mash too hard. Turn off the heat.

Now, set to work on the pastry. Cut it into six equal parts and roll the first piece into a ball in the palms of your hands, then use a rolling pin to roll it into an oval shape, 10cm long and 1mm thick.

Slice the oval in half horizontally to create two half-moons. With the straight edge at the bottom, place a tablespoon of the filling on the first half-moon, positioning it closer to the straight edge. Using wet

Recipe continues on page 130

fingers, bring the two corners up over the filling and pinch together to seal the bottom and make a sort of cone shape. Hold in one hand, with the opening at the top, and push the filling down towards the point. Then pinch the cone closed, folding the curved edge over to create a neat flap. Sit upright on its fat unsealed bottom on the lined baking tray. This is important, as you don't want the samosas to fall over and cook only on one side. You can lean them against ramekins or use a muffin tray instead if you're worried about this.

Continue with the remaining samosas, then chill for 20 minutes while you pre-heat the oven to 200°C/Fan 180°C/Gas 6.

To cook, dot or brush the chilled samosas with the remaining oil and bake for 15–20 minutes. Don't mind too much if they wistfully fall backwards. They'll taste damned good anyway, and you will be too blown away that you made a proper samosa at home to care.

CHILLI CHEESE TOAST

SERVES 4
250g mature Cheddar, grated
1 small onion, finely chopped
4 green or red chillies, roughly chopped
4 slices of bread
Freshly ground black pepper

This cheese on toast spiked with green chillies and onions is a firm favourite from my childhood. Of all the weird and wonderful snacks that arrived on our drinks trolley, these were by far my grandfather's favourite – think Welsh Rarebit with a pungent kick. We Indians can wax lyrical about the perfect recipe for chilli cheese toast, arguing over the addition of a drop of Worcestershire sauce (interesting), whether to bake or grill (debatable) or the inclusion of garlic (contentious).

My mother's recipe is obviously my own preferred method. While she used white sliced bread, you can try slices of French baguette or whatever else you have lying around. Whatever you do, don't cut the crusts off, as they will go crisp, golden and irresistible under the grill.

Pre-heat the grill to high and line a baking sheet with baking parchment.

While the grill is warming up, put the cheese into a bowl. Add the chopped onion and chillies and mix them into the cheese.

Place the bread slices on the lined baking sheet. Spoon equal amounts of the cheesy mixture on top of each slice and finish with a sprinkling of black pepper.

Next shove the baking sheet under the grill until the cheese is golden and bubbling. This will take about 7 minutes, and yes, I do stand in front of the grill and watch the magic happen. Serve this with my Tomato Chilli Instachutney (page 219).

MASALA PAV
BHAJI-STUFFED BREAD ROLLS

MAKES 5–6

FOR THE STUFFING
2 tbsp oil
1 medium onion, thinly sliced
2 tomatoes, roughly chopped
½ tsp ground turmeric
½ tsp ground cumin
¼ tsp garam masala
Salt

FOR THE BREAD ROLLS
2 tsp oil, plus extra for greasing
450–500g ready-made pizza dough
Plain flour, for dusting
1 tbsp whole milk
Nigella and/or white sesame seeds
Softened butter, to finish

While India is probably best known for its flatbreads, we are also lovers of not-so-flat bread. These soft and moreish bread rolls, or *pav*, have a surprise filling of spiced tomato and onion and are popular in continental bakeries in India.

I should confess that I am broadly useless with fancy baking, preferring instead to keep things as simple as possible. This recipe, therefore, uses ready-made pizza dough, which I buy frozen so it's always handy, and a simple twist-and-seal method that should not throw those with a similar skill level to me.

First make the stuffing. Pour the oil into a small frying pan and place over a high heat. When it's hot, add the onion and sauté for 5 minutes, then add the tomatoes and ground spices and cook until the tomatoes disintegrate. Add salt to taste and leave to cool slightly.

Meanwhile, grease a deep, round 20cm cake tin with oil.

Cut the pizza dough into 5–6 equal pieces. Take one piece and place the rest in a bowl, covered with a damp tea towel. Now, roll the ball of dough in your hands or on top of a chopping board until smooth. Dust with flour and then use a rolling pin to flatten it into a rough round shape about 10–12cm in diameter. Plonk a teaspoon of the filling in the middle. Gather up the edges of the dough, then twist and push down to seal. Flip the stuffed bun over and place it in the cake tin.

Repeat until you have all your buns packed tightly into the tin, then cover the tin with the damp tea towel and leave it somewhere warm for 20 minutes. On a cold day, this spot is my oven with just its light on.

When the time is up, take the tin out of the oven while you pre-heat it to 200°C/Fan 180°C/Gas 6. Mix the milk and 2 teaspoons of oil together and use to generously brush the tops of the buns, then scatter the nigella and/or sesame seeds on top.

Gently rub softened butter on the buns for a glossy look before baking for 20 minutes. Serve hot – these really are best eaten straight from the oven but they will keep in an airtight container for up to 2 days.

MACHLI KE CUTLET
FENNEL AND CORIANDER FISHCAKES

MAKES 8–10

500g skinless and boneless white fish
    (frozen or fresh)
300g white potato, peeled and cubed
4 tbsp chopped coriander
2–4 green chillies, finely chopped
4 garlic cloves, finely grated
5cm fresh root ginger, finely grated
2 tbsp lemon juice
1 tbsp ground fennel
1 tbsp ground coriander
1 tsp white pepper
1 tsp salt
Oil, for greasing

These fragrant yet subtly spiced fishcakes are my go-to when I need to make an impression without first undertaking a special shopping trip. I always have bags of sustainable fish and green chillies in the freezer for busy days, so putting these together is easy. Any firm white fish works well here – try cod, pollock, haddock or basa. This recipe uses the grill but you could shallow-fry the fishcakes in batches too. Serve with Hara Chutney (page 216) or Mustard Instachutney (page 219).

Cook the fish until it turns opaque and flakes easily (follow the instructions on the packet if using frozen or poach gently in a pan of milk if using fresh). Boil and drain the potatoes.

Add the coriander, chillies, garlic and ginger to a large bowl along with the lemon juice, fennel, coriander, pepper and salt. Toss in the potatoes and then flake in the fish. Mix well to combine and then stick the mix in the fridge to chill for about half an hour.

When you're ready to cook, pre-heat the grill to high and line a baking sheet with parchment. Divide the mixture into 8–10 equal portions and use your hands to shape each one into a fishcake. Place them on the lined baking sheet and grill for 12 minutes on each side until golden. Serve hot.

NAMAK PARE
NIGELLA AND BLACK PEPPER CRACKERS

SERVES 4–6
70g (½ cup) plain flour
70g (½ cup) chappati flour
½ tsp baking powder
3 tbsp ghee
1 tsp salt
½ tsp freshly ground black pepper
½ tsp nigella seeds

Delicately spiced and crisp, these savoury crackers are a teatime favourite in north India. Usually deep-fried, they are the perfect accompaniment to a strong cup of Masala Chai or aromatic Adrakwali Chai (page 192). Namak Pare (pronounced *par-aye*) also routinely feature as treats cooked at home for Diwali, the Hindu Festival of Lights.

My recipe is for a baked version. While they are traditionally made with plain flour, fine-milled wholewheat chappati flour (*chakki atta*) increases their goodness quotient. The nigella seeds give them a pungent edge; you can also try cumin seeds, carom seeds and crushed dried fenugreek instead. If the crackers don't all disappear in a sitting, store them in an airtight container for up to a week. Enjoy with pickle or slathered with Tomato, Date and Ginger Chutney (page 217).

Pre-heat the oven to 200°C/Fan 180°C/Gas 6.

Put the flours and baking powder into a medium bowl. Add the ghee, salt, black pepper and nigella seeds and rub into the flour with your fingers until you have something that resembles breadcrumbs.

Now add 4–5 tablespoons of cold water, a little at a time, until you can bring together a smooth dough that doesn't get stuck to the edges of the bowl. If you add too much water, just add a teaspoon or two more flour to the dough – it's not a big deal.

Roll the dough out to the thickness of a pound coin on a sheet of baking parchment, then place the rolled dough, with the paper it's sitting on, on a baking sheet. Use a pizza cutter to cut the dough first into strips and then either diamonds or rectangles.

Bake in the oven for 15 minutes. Let the crackers cool slightly before tucking in, or cool completely before storing in an airtight container to enjoy later.

BIG
PLATTERS

INDIANS NEVER KNOWINGLY UNDER-CATER.

Not content with feeding our immediate family, and ourselves, we Indians specialise in feeding large crowds of people. An example of this is the *langar*, or free community kitchen, operated by Gurdwaras (Sikh places of worship), which feed hundreds of people irrespective of caste, religion or social status. Weddings are another case in point: from the poorest families to the wealthiest, this is the mother of all food, drink and fun fests.

On the subject of mothers, mine is a fantastic party thrower. Think professional caterers, a bar brimming with booze and enough nibbles to feed all the invitees plus the rest of the neighbourhood, had they been invited. When I was small, I remember snacks and drinks being served at my parents' parties amidst flares, big hair, disco balls and DJs.

This chapter is all about large-scale Indian hospitality. The recipes serve four, but they can easily be doubled, tripled and even quadrupled to feed a crowd — either as snacks or more filling meals. While you could cook almost any curry in large quantities and serve it up with some naan and pickle, the recipes here promise minimum effort and maximum reward, leaving you to concentrate on being fabulous and having fun. Indian themed canapés, such as Bharwan Kumbh and smoky aubergine Baingan Bharta Bites can all be prepared in advance.

If you fancy something more substantial, the Bombay street food special Pav Bhaji is a great stomach-liner; other street food favourites, such as Jhalmuri and Kala Chana Chaat, double up as DIY party food. When the sun shines, a coal-fired barbecue is a stand-in for a tandoor on which you can make sizzling kebabs.

So put on your glad rags, chill the Prosecco and embrace the spirit of Indian entertaining with the recipes in this chapter.

JHALMURI
PUFFED RICE WITH LIME, NUTS AND CHILLI

SERVES 4

FOR THE TOPPINGS

2 medium potatoes, peeled and diced
50g fresh coconut, cut into 1cm dice
4 tsp chopped coriander
2 green chillies, finely chopped
1 small onion, finely chopped
1 tomato, finely chopped
75g cucumber, finely chopped
4 tsp whole Bengal gram, cooked
4 tsp raw shelled peanuts
Handful of gram flour noodles (sev)

FOR THE MIX

8 large handfuls of puffed rice
2 tsp roasted ground cumin seeds
1 tsp chilli powder
½–1 tsp black salt
4 tsp mustard oil
Juice of 1 lemon or 4 Indian limes
4 tbsp gram flour noodles (sev)

King of all Bengali street food, Jhalmuri is an explosive mix of puffed rice, coconut, peanuts, whole Bengal gram (brown chickpeas) and more, dressed with mustard oil, lime and chilli powder. The name literally translates as 'spicy puffed rice' and it is usually whipped up in a mug – the ingredients laid out on a pick-and-mix station. Puffed rice is sold under its Gujarati name *mamra* by Indian brands, or you can grab a bag of no-added-sugar/salt puffed rice cereal. If you're hitting a specialist ethnic grocery store, look out for potent, fragrant and juicy Indian limes; and while you're there pick up some sev (crispy gram flour noodles), although Bombay mix is an acceptable alternative.

Get all your toppings ready first. Boil the potatoes until soft but still keeping their shape. Arrange the coconut, coriander, chillies, onion, tomato and cucumber in little bowls with the rest of the toppings.

Check whether your puffed rice is still crunchy. If it has softened, toast it in a wok over a medium heat for a couple of minutes to bring it back to life.

Now, toss 2 handfuls of the puffed rice into a large jug. Add ½ teaspoon of the roasted ground cumin, ¼ teaspoon of the chilli powder and black salt to taste; whisk together.

Next add whatever topping you fancy and whisk again. Finish with a teaspoon of the mustard oil and a squeeze of lemon or lime juice. Tip into a bowl, topping with the sev to serve. Then carry on with the next one. If you're not too bothered about customising this, mix all the toppings to your taste in one go. The key here is to taste as you go along to make it perfect for you.

TIP   Consider sprouting your whole Bengal gram for the added health benefits (page 226).

MASALA CHIPS
CHILLI PEANUT INDIAN NACHOS

SERVES 4–6
2 red onions
Large handful of coriander leaves
2 handfuls of peanuts
2–3 green chillies, chopped
Juice of 1 lemon or 4 Indian limes
Salt
150g lightly salted crisps

These crisps topped with lemony onion peanuts are a fine example of sports club food in India. Originally gentlemen's clubs were set up to provide much-needed space for sports and socialising for the British and these relics of the Raj era remain, preserving much old-fashioned charm, anglophilia and a curious assortment of food. Masala Chips were a particular specialty of the Calcutta Swimming Club, which apparently once objected to my grandfather arriving dressed in the traditional Indian loincloth *dhoti*.

The crisps used to make this are typically not of the best quality and soften under the burden of the dressing, adding to the charm of the dish. However, I prefer to buy decent-quality crisps instead, and keep the topping ready to spoon over platters of the crisps as guests arrive. Masala Chips wash down well with a glass of chilled lemon barley soda or, for authenticity, Thums Up cola, but I can vouch for gin and tonic too.

Chop the onion and fresh coriander finely and place in an airtight plastic container. Add the peanuts, chillies, lemon or lime juice and salt to your taste. Stick the lid on and give it a good shake.

When you're ready to serve, spread the crisps on a platter and spoon over the lemony onion mixture.

BAINGAN BHARTA BITES
SMOKY CHARRED AUBERGINE CANAPÉS

MAKES 4–6
2 medium aubergines
3 tbsp oil
1 medium onion, sliced
5cm fresh root ginger, finely grated
1 large tomato, sliced
½ tsp ground turmeric
Handful of coriander, chopped
2 green chillies, finely chopped
Salt
4–6 mini pittas or naan, to serve
Coriander leaves or ginger julienne,
    to garnish (optional)

Moist and moreish, *bharta* simply means a mash of fresh spices and flavourful ingredients. Baingan Bharta is the mother of all bhartas, a smoky, fire-roasted aubergine mash. Spooned onto shop-bought mini pittas or naan, they make perfect Indian canapés.

The aubergine topping doesn't take very long to make and can be prepared in advance. And if you don't want to be fiddling with canapés when your guests arrive, assemble them first and warm them quickly in the microwave before serving.

Pre-heat the oven to 200°C/Fan 180°C/Gas 6.

Rub the aubergines with 1 tablespoon of the oil, then roast them whole in the oven for 30 minutes. You can do this up to 2 days ahead.

Pour the remaining oil into a wok and place over a high heat. When it's hot, tip in the onion and sauté for 5 minutes, then add the ginger and cook for another 5 minutes. Add the sliced tomato, turmeric, coriander (reserving a few leaves to garnish) and green chillies and cook for another 2 minutes until the tomatoes soften. Remove from the heat.

When the aubergines are out of the oven and cool enough to handle by the stem end, turn on the naked flame on your largest hob. Quickly blister each aubergine on either side until you see the skin smoke. Set them aside on a plate until they are cool enough to handle. Then cut off the stems and scoop out the aubergine flesh. Add to the wok and place back over a low-medium heat to bring it to a simmer, mashing with a wooden spoon to remove any large lumps. The end result should have texture but no visible lumps. Season with salt to taste.

Spoon or scoop equal portions onto warmed mini pittas and garnish with coriander leaves or ginger julienne before serving, if liked.

VARIATION ➤ PANEER BHARTA BITES
Instead of the aubergine, mash 500g diced paneer into the spices. Homemade paneer (page 225) works exceptionally well here.

BHARWAN KUMBH
CHEESY STUFFED MUSHROOMS

MAKES 4–5
1 tbsp oil
4 cubes of frozen chopped spinach
4–5 mini Portobello mushrooms
1 medium tomato, diced
1 garlic clove, finely grated
2 tbsp tinned sweetcorn kernels
1 tsp ground coriander
Pinch of chilli powder
Sprinkle of grated nutmeg
4 tbsp grated mature Cheddar
Salt

Sweetcorn, spinach and cheese are an ever-popular combination for continental (or 'Conti') food, the nation's interpretation of European cuisine. Here they form the perfect gently spiced stuffing for mushrooms. Frozen chopped spinach is a boon here as it cooks quickly while you assemble the rest of the ingredients.

Mini Portobello mushrooms make dinky finger foods but you can always double the stuffing and go for full size Portobello mushrooms for a more substantial side. You don't need a dipping sauce as such but a squirt of chilli sauce improves absolutely anything, in my humble opinion.

Pre-heat the grill to high. Line a baking tray with baking parchment and brush lightly with the oil.

Cook the spinach following the packet instructions. While it's cooking, wash and pat dry the mushrooms and remove and finely chop their stalks. Drain the spinach well to squeeze out any excess water.

Mix the tomato and garlic into the cooked spinach in a bowl, along with the chopped mushroom stalks, sweetcorn, coriander, chilli powder, nutmeg and salt to taste.

Place the mushroom caps on the oiled and lined baking tray. Fill with equal amounts of the stuffing, top with the cheese and place under the grill for 7–10 minutes, or until the cheese is melted and golden. Serve warm or cold.

PAV BHAJI
BOMBAY VEGETABLE CURRY WITH BREAD ROLLS

SERVES 4–6

FOR THE PAV BHAJI MASALA
2 tsp coriander seeds
1 tsp cumin seeds
1 tsp fennel seeds
1 tsp whole black peppercorns
1 whole dried red chilli

FOR THE CURRY
300g baking potatoes
1cm fresh root ginger
2 garlic cloves
3 medium tomatoes (about 300g),
    quartered
3 tbsp oil
1 medium onion, finely chopped
1 medium green pepper,
    finely chopped
1 medium carrot, finely chopped
½ tsp ground turmeric
½ tsp Kashmiri chilli powder
    or paprika
125ml (½ cup) hot water
1 tsp garam masala
Generous sprinkle of mango powder
Salt

TO SERVE
Butter
4–6 white bread rolls
Lemon wedges and chopped
    coriander leaves

Pav Bhaji is a tangy, spicy vegetable curry with lashings of butter mopped up with buttered white bread rolls. Mumbai (Bombay), a city infamous for its eye-watering property prices and high cost of living, is also well known for its diverse street food. One of my abiding memories of the city is seeing people from all walks of life standing on street corners as they tuck into delicious snacks.

I wouldn't dream of messing with this sacred recipe, but I do prefer to bake the potatoes instead of boiling them to keep their goodness intact. While ready-made pav bhaji masala is available, making your own means there is no half-used pack left over. Normally you would serve this topped with raw onion, but as this can understandably be unpopular at parties, I have left it out. At any rate, party food doesn't get better than this: you can make it a day in advance, it's filling, packed full of flavour, easy to assemble on the day and any leftovers can be stashed away for a hangover breakfast.

Dry-roast the masala spices in a frying pan set over a medium heat for a minute or two until fragrant. Turn the heat off and leave them to cool down, then remove and discard the chilli stem.

Wash and prick the potatoes for the curry with a fork. Microwave on high for 8–10 minutes until soft, or bake in an oven pre-heated to 220°C/Fan 200°C/Gas 7 for 45 minutes–1 hour.

Use a hand blender to purée the ginger and garlic with a dash of water until smooth, then tip out into a bowl. Add the tomatoes to the blender and purée them too.

Pour the oil into a wok and place over a medium-high heat. When it's hot, toss in the onion and sauté for 2 minutes. Then add the green pepper and carrot. Stir the lot for 5 minutes until soft, then add the puréed ginger and garlic and cook this for another 5 minutes.

Meanwhile, grind the now cool masala spices into a fine powder, using a spice grinder or pestle and mortar. Stir them into the pan along with the turmeric and Kashmiri chilli powder or paprika. Add 2 tablespoons of hot water if the spices start getting stuck to the bottom of the wok.

Now, mix in the puréed tomatoes, lower the heat to a high simmer and let the mixture bubble away for 10 minutes. When oil starts to ooze through the surface, peel and mash the baked potatoes and stir them into the pan, along with the hot water to make a loose curry. Add salt to taste and then sprinkle over the garam masala and mango powder.

To serve, dot the curry with knobs of butter and then butter the bread rolls. Shoving them under a hot grill briefly is recommended, unless you are serving a large crowd. Keep lemon wedges and chopped coriander out for guests to squeeze and sprinkle over as they scoop up the bhaji with their buttered rolls.

BAGHARE BAINGAN

PEANUT, SESAME AND COCONUT AUBERGINES

SERVES 4–6

FOR THE TEMPERING
2 tbsp oil
½ tsp mustard seeds
½ tsp nigella seeds
½ tsp fennel seeds
10–12 curry leaves

FOR THE CURRY
700g baby aubergines
1 medium onion, chopped
1cm fresh root ginger, finely grated
3 garlic cloves, finely grated
4 green chillies, finely chopped
1 tsp ground coriander
½ tsp chilli powder
½ tsp ground turmeric
3 tbsp smooth peanut butter
    (with no added sugar or salt)
1 × 400ml tin coconut milk
    (at least 75% coconut)
1 tbsp tahini
1 tsp tamarind paste
Salt
Small handful of peanuts,
    roughly crushed, to garnish

Roasted aubergines slathered in a peanut, sesame and coconut curry is one of my most popular party dishes, and it's no surprise why. This regal dish is most closely associated with the Hyderabadi Nizams, the Mughal administrators who declared their independence as the Empire crumbled. Without their rebellion we may have never experienced the tantalising Hyderabadi cuisine.

Baghare means 'tempered', so the name of the recipe actually refers to the spice tempering. Despite the long list of ingredients, this is actually a very simple recipe using storecupboard basics: tinned coconut milk, peanut butter and tahini. Serve with flatbreads for scooping up the curry.

First soak the aubergines in a large bowl of cold salted water for at least 1 hour. Pre-heat the oven to 200°C/Fan 180°C/Gas 6 and line a baking tray with baking parchment.

Drain the aubergines and pat dry with kitchen paper. Make slits in them, keeping the tops intact, and roast on the tray for 20 minutes.

Meanwhile, temper the spices. Pour the oil into a wok or heavy-based pan and place over a medium-high heat. When it's hot, toss in the seeds and the curry leaves. As they sizzle up, add the onion and cook for 5 minutes, stirring to coat in the spices. Then add the ginger, garlic and green chillies and cook for another 5 minutes. Now add the coriander, chilli powder and turmeric and stir well for a couple of minutes. If the spice mixture start getting stuck to the bottom of the pan, add a few tablespoons of hot water and scrape it off.

If your peanut butter is a little stiff, give it a mix with some of the coconut milk in a hand blender before adding it to the pan, along with the rest of the coconut milk and the tahini. Cook for 5 minutes at a high simmer, then stir in the tamarind paste and add salt to taste.

Finally drop the roasted aubergines into the pan and spoon the curry over them. Serve with a smattering of roughly crushed peanuts.

KALA CHANA CHAAT
CHUTNEYED BROWN CHICKPEA SALAD

SERVES 4–6

FOR THE CHAAT
2 large potatoes (about 500g), peeled
   and diced
4 large handfuls of whole Bengal gram,
   cooked
1 small onion, finely chopped
150g cucumber, diced
20–30 papdi or savoury crackers,
   broken into bite-sized pieces
   (optional)
4 tbsp pomegranate seeds
8 tsp crispy gram flour noodles (sev)
Handful of chopped coriander

FOR THE TAMARIND CHUTNEY
Kettle of freshly boiled water
5cm ball of tamarind
2 tsp brown sugar
¼ tsp freshly ground black pepper
½ tsp black salt

FOR THE CHAAT MASALA
1 tsp cumin seeds
¼ tsp freshly ground black pepper
½ tsp ground coriander
¼ tsp ground ginger
½ tsp black salt
½ tsp mango powder
¼ tsp chilli powder

FOR THE GREEN CHUTNEY
Large handful of coriander leaves
2 mint sprigs, leaves picked
2 green chillies
Juice of 1 lemon
½ tsp sugar
Salt

A whole Bengal gram (brown chickpea) and potato salad smothered in spiky coriander and sour tamarind chutneys and then finished with warm, earthy spices, this Chaat is a flavour bomb that will explode in your mouth. *Chaat* means 'to lick', and that's precisely what you will want to do to the bowl after you finish. Served all over India in many different versions, this is street food at its best.

Sprout your own whole Bengal gram (page 226) or use tinned cooked brown chickpeas to save time. Look out for crackers called papdi in ethnic stores for added crunch; RW Garcia's 3-seed crackers are an excellent substitute.

Boil the potatoes for 5 minutes until soft but still keeping their shape. Drain, reserving the water for the tamarind chutney, and set aside to cool.

To make the tamarind chutney, pour the reserved hot liquid into a heavy-based pan, topping it up with hot water from the kettle if needed to get 500ml (2 cups). Add the tamarind, bring to the boil, then lower the heat to a high simmer and bubble for 10 minutes until thick. Strain into a bowl, pressing the tamarind pulp well to extract as much as possible. Using a spoon, scoop the tamarind from under the sieve back into the bowl. Add the sugar, black pepper and black salt, mix thoroughly and set aside to cool.

Now, on to the chaat masala. Dry-roast the cumin seeds in a small pan over a medium heat for 30 seconds. Then grind to a fine powder using a pestle and mortar or spice grinder. Tip into a bowl and add all the other chaat masala spices. Stir through until well combined, breaking up any lumps.

Next, make the green chutney. Wash the herbs and then purée until smooth in a hand blender with the chillies, lemon juice and sugar. Add salt to your taste – a teaspoon does it for me.

    Recipe continues on page 152

Now, it's simply an assembly job. Pile the whole Bengal gram and potatoes into a serving dish and scatter over the chopped onion, cucumber and papdi or crackers, if using. Spoon over a couple of tablespoons of the tamarind chutney first, then drizzle over the green chutney. Add a generous sprinkling of the chaat masala and finally the pomegranate seeds, crispy gram flour noodles and chopped coriander. Enjoy immediately.

TIP   If you're going to the trouble of making chutney, always make extra and store it in the fridge to enjoy as dips, sandwich stuffing or salad dressing. You could also throw a *chaat* party – where you serve a combination of Kala Chana Chaat and Jhalmuri (page 140). That's effort well made!

ALOO BOTI KEBAB
SIZZLED SIRLOIN, POTATO AND ONION SKEWERS

MAKES 6–8 SKEWERS
650g thick-cut sirloin steak
2 tbsp natural yoghurt
1 tbsp grated fresh root ginger
1 tbsp grated garlic
1 tbsp white vinegar
½ tsp chilli powder
1 generous tbsp garam masala
6–8 new potatoes, cut into 1cm slices
1 large onion, cut into chunks
1 tbsp oil
1 tsp salt

These super-simple and highly flavourful skewers are great shoved on the barbecue or cooked under a hot grill. Said to have originated in the campsites of Persian soldiers where they were threaded onto swords, Boti Kebabs are now cooked on slightly less menacing metal or bamboo skewers. My version uses sirloin steak and a very Indian homemaker trick to make portions stretch a little more: bulk, by way of new potatoes and onions. You can use cubed lamb leg steaks instead of sirloin, if you prefer.

So simple is this recipe, that you may consider making your own fresh garam masala (page 227). Serve the kebabs with a fresh salad, like Muttakoos Thoran (page 167).

Dice the sirloin into 2.5cm cubes then add to a bowl with the yoghurt, ginger, garlic, vinegar, chilli powder and garam masala and stir until well combined. Place in the fridge to marinate for 2–4 hours. If you are using wooden or bamboo skewers instead of metal ones, soak them in water during this time.

When you're ready to cook, bring the marinated steak to room temperature and pre-heat the grill to high.

Thread the potato, onion and beef onto the skewers evenly, leaving a small gap around the meat cubes. When they're all done, brush with the oil and sprinkle salt on them. Cook on a baking tray under the hot grill for 10 minutes on one side, then flip over and cook for another 10 minutes.

Alternatively, you can barbecue the kebabs over hot coals for about 20 minutes, turning them regularly, until the potatoes are cooked and the beef is soft.

CALCUTTA KATI ROLLS
LEMONY CHILLI CHICKEN KEBAB WRAPS

SERVES 4–6

600g skinless chicken thigh fillets, cut into large chunks

3 small red onions, thinly sliced

3–4 green chillies, chopped

Juice of 1 lemon

4–6 parathas, shop-bought or homemade (page 176)

Large handful of coriander leaves

FOR THE MARINADE

125g Greek-style yoghurt

4 garlic cloves, finely grated

2.5cm fresh root ginger, finely grated

2 tsp ground coriander

2 tsp ground cumin

2 tsp Kashmiri chilli powder or paprika

½ tsp chilli powder

1 tsp ground turmeric

1 tsp garam masala

2 tbsp mustard oil

Salt

An iconic bit of Calcutta street food, these paratha wraps enclose cubes of marinated chicken and lemony chilli-spiked onions. The juicy filling is guaranteed to drip down your chin as the flavours run riot in your mouth with every bite.

The kebab filling is usually skewered on a *kati* or stick, and cooked in a tandoor oven, but this is an oven-friendly recipe. If you have tandoori marinade (page 158) lying around, feel free to use it instead of the one given here. Ready-made fresh or frozen parathas will make a breeze of this recipe, although packs of rotis warmed with a little ghee will also do.

Put the yoghurt into a large bowl and add all the other marinade ingredients, adding salt to taste. Toss the chicken pieces into the marinade, mix well to coat and leave to sit for 1 hour. If you are using wooden or bamboo skewers instead of metal ones, soak them in water during this time.

Meanwhile, drench the onions and chillies in the lemon juice.

When you're ready to cook, pre-heat the grill to high. Thread the chicken onto the skewers and place on a rack directly under the grill with a baking tray underneath to catch the dripping juices. Cook the chicken for 20–25 minutes, turning the skewers two or three times. You could simply shove the kebabs on a barbecue, if you prefer.

While the chicken is cooking, make or warm your parathas, following the instructions on the packet.

Now, it's just an assembly job. Take a paratha, top with a generous amount of the onion-chilli mixture, some coriander leaves and then a few pieces of chicken. Fold the edge of the paratha in where the last chicken piece sits, then fold one long edge over, roll the lot up like a wrap and tuck in.

VARIATION ➤ PANEER BHURJI ROLLS
For vegetarians in your midst, make Paneer Bhurji (page 92) as an alternative filling.

GALINHA CAFREAL
GOAN CORIANDER CHICKEN

SERVES 4–6

5cm cinnamon stick

6 cloves

1 tbsp coriander seeds

1 tbsp cumin seeds

100g bunch of coriander

6cm fresh root ginger, roughly chopped

8 garlic cloves, roughly chopped

4 green chillies, roughly chopped

4 tbsp coconut vinegar

8 skinless bone-in chicken thighs

4 tbsp oil

Salt

Spicy, sour and fragrant with heady fresh coriander, this is Goa's answer to tandoori chicken. It is said to have been introduced by Portuguese colonialists. (*Galinha*, in fact, is chicken in Portuguese.)

You can cook this in several different ways, always using the same marinade, as I discovered on a recent trip to Goa. My preferred method is to roast as below, although it is also excellent cooked on a barbecue on warmer days.

Dry-roast the cinnamon stick, cloves, coriander and cumin seeds in a small frying pan for 30 seconds over a medium heat. When the spices are fragrant, remove from the heat and leave to cool.

Cut off the bottom 5cm of the coriander stalks and discard. Working in two batches, add the coriander to a small hand blender or food processor with the ginger, garlic, chillies, coconut vinegar and roasted spices. Blitz until you get a smooth paste, then add salt to taste.

Now line a baking tray that will fit the chicken thighs without overcrowding. Slather the green paste all over them, put into the fridge and leave the marinade to work its magic for at least 1 hour – the vinegar will do wonders to tenderise the chicken.

When you're ready to cook, pre-heat the oven to 190°C/Fan 170°C/Gas 5 and drizzle the oil over the chicken. Loosely cover the baking tray with foil and place it in the centre of the oven. Cook the chicken for 45–50 minutes, basting once halfway through cooking. Test a piece to check if it's cooked through – the juices from the centre should run clear.

TANDOORI JHINGA
SMOKY CHARRED PUNJABI PRAWNS

SERVES 4–6
1kg large raw king prawns,
    shell and head on
4 tbsp oil
Juice of ½ lemon

FOR THE TANDOORI MARINADE
4 tsp coriander seeds
2 tsp cumin seeds
8 garlic cloves
5cm fresh root ginger
125g Greek-style yoghurt
1 tsp dried fenugreek leaves
1 tsp garam masala
½ tsp ground turmeric
½ tsp chilli powder
1 tbsp Kashmiri chilli powder
    or paprika
1 tsp salt

These smoky and fragrant kebabs are a mainstay of Punjabi cooking. 'Tandoori' gets its name from the tandoor, a charcoal-fired oven with clay walls that cooks flatbreads and kebabs with precision. In many restaurants tandoori marinade gets its characteristic Day-Glo red appearance from a dash of artificial colour, but Kashmiri chilli powder or paprika is used more commonly at home.

Always add the marinade to your prawns rather than the other way around so you can squirrel away any leftover marinade. It keeps for up to 2 weeks in the fridge – try it on skewered chunks of paneer, button mushrooms or chicken (see below).

First make the marinade. In a small pan, dry-roast the coriander and cumin seeds for 30 seconds over a medium heat, then remove from the heat and leave to cool.

Using a hand blender, purée the garlic and ginger to a smooth paste with 2–3 tablespoons of the yoghurt, the fenugreek leaves and roasted spices. Tip this paste into a bowl and mix in the rest of the marinade ingredients.

Rinse and pat dry the prawns, keeping the heads and tails intact. Drench them in the marinade and leave to sit in the fridge for 2 hours.

When you're ready to cook, pre-heat the grill to its highest setting or fire up your barbecue. For really large prawns, brush with the oil and lemon juice and then either grill or barbecue for 5 minutes. For smaller prawns, thread them onto skewers and brush with the oil and lemon juice before grilling for 4–5 minutes.

VARIATION ➤ TANDOORI MURGH
For tandoori chicken, mix the marinade and 1 tablespoon of papaya enzyme (page 237) into 4 skinned, slashed chicken legs. Marinate for 4 hours, then grill on a barbecue for 30 minutes, turning and basting with oil and lemon juice. You can also roast the chicken in an oven pre-heated to 200°C/Fan 180°C/Gas 6; place it directly on an oven shelf with a lined tray underneath to catch the drips. Cook for 45 minutes, turning twice.

SIDE
DISHES

IN INDIA, WE DON'T TREAT ACCOMPANIMENTS AS AFTERTHOUGHTS.

Side dishes often complete a meal and are almost as important as the main dish. The Keralan *sadhya*, for instance, which literally means 'banquet' or 'feast', is traditionally served at lunch and casually comprises anywhere between 10 and 65 vegetarian side dishes on a banana leaf.

This chapter features vegetarian recipes to accompany most meals, including traditional carb options such as fluffy rice and flatbreads. You'll find top tips to ensure you get perfectly soft rotis, and a layered paratha that is practically idiot-proof. The naan is an instant version that doesn't need to prove, so you can add it to elaborate dishes like Ma Ki Dal (page 64) for an effortless meal.

Continuing on the traditional theme are my dal and raita recipes, which you can add to spicy meals or dishes that don't have curry to balance flavours and add textural variety. When you're not in the mood for a full-blown meal, add the Muttakoos Thoran (cabbage, coconut and curry leaf slaw) to Chepa Vepudu (page 52) or stir-fry a larger portion of Sukhi Bhaji for a lightweight meal filled with aromatic goodness.

So whether you are preparing an elaborate meal or a quick weekday fix, this chapter has everything you need to complete it. Keep pickle and papad handy, and satisfaction is guaranteed.

PERFECT BASMATI

SERVES 4
270g (1½ cups) basmati rice
680ml (2¾ cups) hot water

No self-respecting Indian cookbook is complete without a technique for making perfect fluffy rice. The journey invariably starts with the best quality basmati – the foothills of the Himalayas in the north of India and Pakistan provide the perfect topography for growing this slender, long and aromatic grain. Look out for long-grain varieties, which make an extra visual impact when cooked.

You could, of course, always use a rice cooker to get pitch perfect results every time. If you do decide to buy one, choose a brand local to a rice-loving nation – mine is Iranian. But if you fancy doing things the old-fashioned, manual way, this method won't fail.

First tip the rice into a sieve and wash it thoroughly under the cold tap until the water runs clear. You can cup your hand under the sieve to check.

Put the rice into a medium pan, add the hot water and bring to a rapid boil over a high heat.

When the water starts bubbling, lower the heat to a high simmer, cover and cook for 12–15 minutes without lifting the lid to sneak a peek (12 minutes for regular basmati, 15 minutes for long-grain varieties). The heat needs to be high enough for the rice to cook. When the time is up, remove from the heat, leaving the lid on.

Cooked basmati straight out of the pan disintegrates easily so leave it to sit, covered, for at least 5 minutes before you remove the lid. Loosen the grains with a fork before serving.

SABZI PULAO

SPICED VEGETABLE-STUDDED BASMATI

SERVES 4

270g (1½ cups) basmati rice

1 medium carrot, 10 green beans and
a handful of peas (or use 1½ cups
frozen chopped mixed vegetables)

1½ tbsp ghee

1cm fresh root ginger, finely grated

1 large bay leaf

1 tsp cumin seeds

1 star anise

5cm cinnamon stick

¾ tsp ground turmeric (optional)

1½ tsp salt

680ml (2¾ cups) hot water

TO GARNISH (OPTIONAL)

Handful of raw cashews

1 tbsp ghee

1 small onion, thinly sliced

Pinch of sugar

Pinch of salt

Pulao is delicately spiced basmati rice that is sautéed and then steamed until the grains are cooked to perfection – not to be confused with *biryani*, which is a lavish, aromatic preparation of layered rice and meat. The yellow hue provided by the turmeric is entirely up to you and the palette of the meal you are serving. As for the garnish, you can forgo it entirely unless you fancy a showstopper effect.

There are three tricks to remember when making perfect pulao. First, wash the rice really well to rid it of starch. Second, use the right amount of hot water – just under two cups of hot water to every cup of rice. And finally, strictly no peeking once the lid goes on the pan.

Wash the rice thoroughly in a sieve under the cold tap until the water runs clear. If using fresh vegetables, peel the carrot and chop it into small dice along with the green beans.

Put the ghee into a large pan, place over a medium-high heat and, when it's hot, add the ginger, bay leaf, cumin seeds, star anise, cinnamon stick and turmeric, if using. As they start sizzling, stir through the fresh vegetables (if using frozen, reserve them for later), then the rice and salt.

Stir for another minute until the rice starts turning bright white. Now add the hot water and frozen vegetables, if using. Quickly bring to the boil and then lower the heat to a high simmer. Cover and steam for 12–15 minutes, or until the rice is cooked and the water has all been absorbed. Remove from the heat and leave the rice to sit for 5 minutes before you take the lid off.

If you're creating the garnish, first dry-roast the cashews in a small frying pan over a medium heat. Tip out of the pan and add the ghee to the same pan. Add the sliced onion, sugar and salt and caramelise over a medium-high heat. Just before serving your pulao, top with the caramelised onions and toasted cashews.

ZAFRANI ALOO
SAFFRON ROAST POTATOES

SERVES 4–6

3 tbsp whole milk
½ tsp saffron threads
750g medium potatoes, peeled
    and quartered
2 tbsp oil
2 pinches of ground turmeric
Salt

A twist on Sunday lunch roast potatoes, these golden yellow beauties get their bright hue from the turmeric and their subtle fragrance from the saffron. They are the perfect accompaniment to Mughlai Murgh Musallam (page 74) and Sikandari Raan (page 80), but you can serve them with pretty much anything you fancy.

Pre-heat the oven to 200°C/Fan 180°C/Gas 6 and line a baking tray with foil or baking parchment.

Warm the milk in a small pan, then remove from the heat and soak the saffron threads in it.

Put the potatoes into a large pan of cold water. Bring them to a quick boil, then drain and return to the pan.

Now, pour the oil and saffron, along with its milk, into the potatoes. Mix in the turmeric, add salt to taste and shake the pan to bash the outside of the potatoes – this will give you a crunchier end result.

Place the potatoes on the lined tray, rounded sides down, and roast for 1 hour, turning once halfway through cooking.

MUTTAKOOS THORAN

CABBAGE, COCONUT AND CURRY LEAF SLAW

SERVES 4
200g (½ small) red cabbage
200g (½ small) white cabbage
200g fresh coconut
2 tbsp coconut oil
2 green chillies
15 curry leaves
2 shallots, thinly sliced
Juice of 2 limes, plus more to taste
Salt

Shredded cabbage gets a complete makeover when tossed in a subtle coconut, lime, curry leaf and green chilli dressing. While the cooked version of this Keralan vegetable stir fry is better known, I discovered the fresh salad version below at George and Sumi's gorgeous Villa De Parrai in Kerala's Alleppey backwaters. In the absence of the villa's garden-fresh curry leaves and coconut, gently warming the coconut oil will help enhance the flavours.

This recipe requires little more than vegetable shredding and ingredient tossing. With the know-how firmly in place, you can adapt it with other varieties of cabbage, lettuce, carrot or beetroot. Use fresh or freshly frozen coconut instead of the desiccated variety as it really does make a difference here.

Thinly shred the red and white cabbage using a sharp knife, mandoline or the grater attachment in your food processor. Peel off the brown, hard outer peel of the coconut and then shred it in a hand blender.

Warm the coconut oil in a wok or large pan over a low heat. Slice the green chillies into three on the diagonal and add them to the oil, along with the curry leaves, for a minute. Turn the heat off and tip in the cabbage, coconut and shallots.

Squeeze over the lime juice and toss the salad, preferably with your hands, to mix thoroughly. Taste and adjust the seasoning, adding salt and more lime juice if you think it needs it. Cover and leave for 20 minutes for the flavours to mingle before serving.

SUKHI BHAJI
SIMPLY STIR-FRIED TENDERSTEM AND BEANS

SERVES 4
300g tenderstem broccoli
200g green beans
4 tbsp oil
¼ tsp asafoetida
1 tsp cumin seeds
1 tsp mustard seeds
10 curry leaves (optional)
1 tsp chilli powder
¼ tsp ground turmeric (optional)
Salt
Coriander leaves and lemon
    or lime wedges, to garnish

This recipe is the perfect go-to when you need a vegetarian dish fast, with the full impact of sizzled whole spices. It hails from the western state of Gujarat, which has a great tradition of veganism and vegetarianism. In their Sukhi Bhaji, or 'dry fry', asafoetida is used to infuse the vegetables with its onion and garlic flavour.

This dish can liven up a thali but it also makes a great stand-in for rice or flatbreads in a low-carb weekday meal. Experiment with the vegetables and put whatever you have in your fridge to exotic use. Any leftovers are handy for toastie stuffing, especially if you've made one of the two variations using potatoes below.

Wash the vegetables, halving the beans if you want. Slit the hard ends of the tenderstem stalks to speed up the cooking time.

Pour the oil into a wok and place over a medium-high heat. When it's hot, drop in the asafoetida and then quickly add the cumin seeds, mustard seeds and curry leaves, if using. As they sizzle up, toss in the broccoli and green beans one at a time. As a rule of thumb, the larger vegetables will take longer to cook, so add them first.

Sprinkle in the chilli powder and turmeric, if using, and mix into the vegetables. Then stick the lid on and cook, stirring from time to time until the vegetables are cooked through. Season with salt and garnish with coriander and lemon or lime wedges.

VARIATIONS

> BHINDI ALOO
Use 350g okra with 2 medium peeled and cubed potatoes instead of the broccoli and beans. Wash the uncut okra in cold water first, then dry thoroughly before slicing to remove all traces of slime.

> BAINGAN ALOO
Use 350g diced aubergines, soaked in cold water for 1 hour, cooked with 12 quartered new potatoes instead of the broccoli and beans. Garnish with chopped dill instead of coriander.

SHAAG BHAJA

DAILY GREENS IN CHILLI GARLIC OIL

SERVES 4

400g fresh greens of your choice, washed
2 tbsp mustard oil
6 garlic cloves, sliced in half
4–6 whole dried red chillies
Salt

Stir-fried greens are an important part of meals in India, where they are enjoyed alongside dal and rice, or in the case of Bengal, at the start of the meal mixed into steamed rice. This recipe is for the simple sauté with garlic and chillies that we enjoyed every day when I was a child. While this completes any full Indian meal I can attest that it's also excellent with baked or shallow-fried fish, such as Chepa Vepudu (page 52) or Bhapa Maach (page 48).

You can use any greens here – kale, spinach, chard, spring greens and savoy cabbage all work well. Look out for a favourite of mine, red amaranth, which will also stain your rice a pretty pink. Replace the mustard oil with another oil of your choice if you prefer, or toss half a teaspoon of panch phoron (Bengali five-spice) or nigella seeds in the hot oil.

Discard any hard stalks or ends from your greens and roughly shred or slice them.

Pour the mustard oil into a wok and place over a high heat. When it's hot, drop in the garlic and whole dried red chillies. As they sizzle up, stir through the greens. Cook, stirring, for 4–5 minutes until the greens wilt.

Season to taste with salt and serve.

TADKA DAL
RED LENTILS WITH SIZZLING SPICES

SERVES 4
185g (1 cup) red split lentils
1 tsp oil
½ tsp ground turmeric
Full kettle of freshly boiled water
Salt

FOR THE TADKA
1 generous tsp ghee
Pinch of asafoetida
1½ tsp cumin seeds
4 whole dried red chillies
½ tsp chilli powder

Lentils, stewed and then topped with sizzling aromatic spices, is a staple accompaniment to most Indian meals. Tadka, pronounced *ter-ka*, describes the tempered spices, but it is also known as *vaghar*, *chaunk*, *phoron* and more. This recipe is from my mother's family home in Delhi.

Although the family version uses yellow lentils, red lentils can be easier to source. A dash of ghee in this is non-negotiable. The most time-consuming part of making dal is bubbling it with the slow addition of hot water to get the lentils to soften into a smooth, soup-like texture. Make extra dal and freeze some for days when you need a hug in a bowl. Serve piping hot with a bowl of steaming basmati or rotis, for dunking.

Wash the red lentils in a sieve under the cold tap until the water runs clear. Then drain and put into a medium pan with enough cold water to completely submerge them – about 375ml (1½ cups).

Add the oil to the water and bring it to a rolling boil over a medium-high heat. Foam will rise to the surface – just skim it off with a ladle.

When you've managed to get rid of most of the foam, stir in the turmeric. Keep it bubbling, adding 125ml (½ cup) hot water whenever when it starts spitting. In about 20 minutes, you'll get a soup-like consistency with no visible whole lentils. Season to taste with salt, lower the heat and allow the lentils to simmer, uncovered.

Next make the tadka. Put the ghee into a small pan and place over a medium heat. Add the asafoetida, then quickly toss in the cumin seeds, red chillies and chilli powder. As they sizzle up, stir this through your dal. Your dal will have thickened as it waits, so feel free to add another 125ml (½ cup) hot water to loosen it up.

VARIATION ➤ MASOOR KI TADKA DAL
Transform this dal by bubbling it with 2 peeled garlic cloves and 2cm fresh root ginger. Add ½ teaspoon mustard seeds and 15 curry leaves to the sizzling tadka. *Recipe pictured on the cover.*

COCONUT DAL

SERVES 4

185g (1 cup) red split lentils
2 tbsp oil
2 medium onions, thinly sliced
4 garlic cloves, finely grated
½ tsp chilli powder
1½ tsp paprika
1½ tsp ground cumin
Full kettle of freshly boiled water
1 × 400ml tin coconut milk
   (at least 75% coconut)
1 tsp sugar
1 tbsp white vinegar
1 tsp Worcestershire sauce
Salt

The perfect antidote to a spicy meal, this creamy and subtle dal hails from the Parsi community. The Persian Zoroastrians first arrived in Gujarat where they adopted the state's love of sweet and sour into their own cuisine. I first discovered it in Jeroo Mehta's *101 Parsi Recipes*, my introduction to cooking the community's incredible cuisine, in which it is described as 'an unusual way to cook lentils'.

With Worcestershire sauce and vinegar accompanying the coconut milk that goes into it, this dal really is unusual. While red lentils (*masoor*) are more typical, you can replace them with skinless yellow lentils. It goes very well with Jungli Maas (page 77) and Vindaloo Pulled Pork (page 86).

Wash the lentils in a sieve under the cold tap until the water runs clear, then leave them to sit.

Pour the oil into a medium pan and place over a high heat. When it's hot, add the onions and sauté for 5 minutes until softened. Add the garlic and stir through for another 5 minutes until golden. Now, tip in the chilli powder, paprika and cumin. Sauté this for another 2 minutes, adding a splash of water if it starts sticking to the bottom of the pan.

Next, stir the lentils into the pan. Add 750ml (3 cups) hot water and bring to the boil, then cook over a medium-high heat for 20 minutes, stirring regularly. If the dal dries up too much and starts hissing and spitting, you can add another cup of water.

When the time is up, lower the heat to low-medium and stir in the coconut milk, sugar, vinegar and Worcestershire sauce. Season with salt to taste and simmer for 5 minutes. While it's simmering, use the wooden spoon to smash the lentils against the sides of the pan to get a smoother texture. Serve hot.

NAAN

INSTANT PILLOWY FLATBREAD

MAKES 2 LARGE OR
4 SMALL NAANS

250g (1½ cups) plain flour
1 tsp baking powder
4 tbsp Greek-style yoghurt
1 tsp salt
1 tsp sugar
2½ tbsp oil, plus more if needed
160–180ml hand-hot whole milk
Smattering of sesame or nigella seeds
Butter

The mainstay of north Indian bread baskets, naan is characterised by pillowy bubbles of trapped air topped with dark golden spots. Watching experienced tandoor chefs make this is a joy to behold – so pliable is the dough that they don't even roll it out, merely stretching it to the desired shape in their hands before smacking it on the hot tandoor oven.

As I have so far resisted erecting my own tandoor oven, my version is a quick fix that can be cooked under a hot grill, with no yeast or proving needed. Using flour to help roll these is strictly banned as it makes for harder naan.

Put the flour and baking powder into a large bowl and add the yoghurt, salt, sugar and 2 tablespoons of the oil. Mix well, adding the warm milk a little at a time, until you get a sticky but well incorporated dough with no loose flour left in the bowl. Put the remaining oil into the hand you are using to mix the dough and then bring the dough together using your oiled hand. If it's too wet, add a bit more plain flour.

Cover the bowl with a clean, slightly damp tea towel and leave it to sit for 15 minutes. Pre-heat the grill to its highest setting and slide a baking sheet under it to warm up.

Divide the dough into two or four equal portions. Shape one piece into a teardrop shape on a clean worktop, leaving the remaining dough covered. If it sticks, dot a bit of oil on it. Using gentle pressure, quickly roll the dough out to a thickness of 5mm, sprinkling the seeds on top and pushing them into the dough.

Line the hot baking sheet with a large sheet of baking parchment and lift the flatbread onto it. Shove under the hot grill for 3–3½ minutes. The top will bubble up and develop brown spots in places. Take out, brush with butter and get started on the next one. Keep them warm and soft by wrapping in a tea towel lined with foil.

TIP   The naan can also be made in advance. To reheat, pat them with damp kitchen paper and then either microwave for 30 seconds or heat on a warm flat griddle or frying pan for 10 seconds on each side.

PARATHA
LAYERED WHOLEWHEAT FLATBREADS

MAKES 4

60ml (¼ cup) whole milk

175g (1 heaped cup) plain flour

3 tbsp chappati flour

1 tsp salt

1 tsp sugar

2 tbsp oil, plus more as needed

1 tbsp milled seeds, such as hemp,
  chia or linseed (optional)

Parathas are shallow-fried flatbreads, best teamed with pickles. As every Indian home needs a dependable paratha recipe, mine uses a simple triangle-fold method, one that is used both in Delhi and Bengal. It can be rolled out any which way as long as it maintains a semblance of a triangle.

This recipe uses a small amount of wholewheat chappati flour in the dough to prevent it from springing back too much when rolling to make it easier to manoeuvre. The key to getting a super-soft end result is warm liquid (to bring the flour together), sticky dough that seems impossible to mould initially and absolutely no flour sprinkled during rolling.

Add water to the milk to bring it up to 125ml (½ cup) and then warm it to hand-hot temperature. I do this in the microwave for ease.

Put both flours into a non-metallic bowl and add the salt, sugar, 1 tablespoon of the oil and the milled seeds, if using. Mix with your fingers and then stir in the watery milk, a little at a time, until you get soggy dough that looks like it will be impossible to roll out.

Cover the bowl with a damp tea towel and leave to sit in a warm place for half an hour. When the time is up, mix the remaining tablespoon of oil into the dough, squeezing and punching it well. Then divide into four equal balls. Cover again and leave to sit for another 10 minutes.

Now, place a well-seasoned flat griddle or heavy-based frying pan over a high heat. When it's hot, lower the heat to medium. While it's warming up, roll out one dough ball into the best circle you can manage. Dot with a little oil, fold it in half, then dot with more oil and fold again to make a little triangle. Roll out the triangle out thinly to get a layered paratha.

The dough will try to spring back, so work quickly and smack it onto the pan to cook. Cook for about a minute on each side, applying pressure with a spatula to the thick edges to help them cook. When the translucent bits of the paratha disappear, set it aside on a plate, covered with a tea towel, and crack on with the next one. Repeat until you have four parathas.

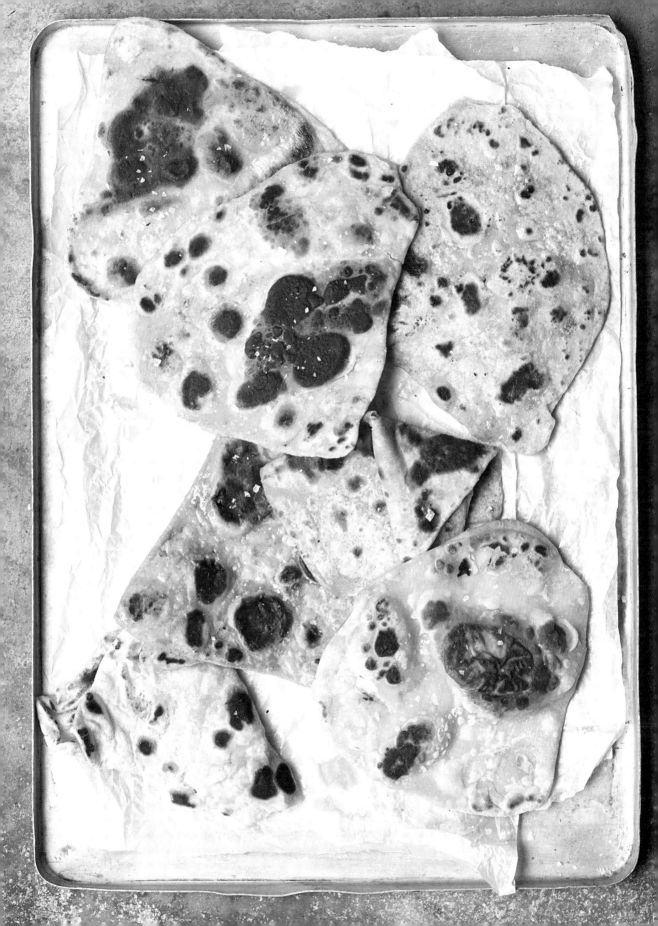

ROTI
PAN-ROASTED WHOLEWHEAT FLATBREADS

MAKES 8

175g (1½ cups) chappati flour, plus extra for rolling and dusting
1 tbsp oil
½ tsp salt
190ml (¾ cup) hand-hot water
Butter or ghee (optional)

Soft, fluffy and pan-roasted, roti is our daily bread, especially in the north and west of India. Made with fine wholewheat chappati flour, these flatbreads provide a steady and slow release of energy – the perfect fuel for busy workers in fields, factories and offices.

There are two kinds of roti – chappati and phulka. Chappatis are dry-roasted on a flat griddle and get their name from their flat (*chappa*) surface with bubbles of trapped air, while phulkas are lifted onto an open fire after a brief moment on the griddle to swell up like balloons. The recipe here is for the easier chappati version. A dash of oil softens the chappatis, but if you keep practising your chappati-making skills, you may reach the Holy Grail of Rotis – impossibly thin, perfectly round roti with no oil involved!

Put the flour into a bowl and make a well in the middle. Pour the oil into the well and sprinkle the salt all over. Now, slowly add the warm water, using your fingers to turn the mixture first into crumbs and then a soft and sticky dough with all the flour incorporated. It's important to add the water slowly as this will make the chappatis soft, although if you add too much water, just tip in a bit more flour. It's okay to end up with slightly sticky, soft dough as it will firm up.

When it's ready, cover the bowl with a damp tea towel and leave to sit for 10–15 minutes.

Next, turn out the dough onto a clean chopping board or worktop and give it a good pummelling, knocking it with your knuckles and pushing it down with your palms. Do this for at least 5 minutes, more if your arms allow. You will end up with soft and pliable dough that springs back when prodded. Now, divide the dough into eight equal balls and return to the bowl to sit, covered, while you get everything ready. Place 2–3 tablespoons of chappati flour in a shallow bowl and get a rolling pin and chopping board out. Set a flat griddle or large heavy-based frying pan over a medium heat and keep a flat spatula handy. Place a clean tea towel on a warmed plate and cover it with foil for the prepared hot chappatis to sit on.

Leaving the others covered, turn the first dough ball into a perfect round by rolling it in your palms or on the board. Dip it in the flour, flattening it slightly, then place it on your board.

Roll the chappati out with a rolling pin to a thickness of 1–2mm, applying even and gentle pressure. The best way to get the perfect round shape is to keep turning it clockwise as you roll. Sprinkle more flour if your rolling pin starts getting stuck to the dough. Roll it out evenly – smoothing your hand over the surface usually reveals any lumpy bits.

Then lift it up, dusting off the excess flour by patting the roti on your hands, and place on the hot griddle or pan. As soon as little bubbles appear, flip the chappati and gently press the edges with a flat spatula for 30 seconds to encourage the bubbles to form. Flip over one more time for a few seconds, then remove and place on your foil-lined plate. You can dab it with butter or ghee, or not – entirely up to you.

Now get cracking with the next one. When you're relatively expert at this, you will be able to roll the next roti while the first one is cooking. When the chappatis are all done, fold over the foil and the tea towel to keep them warm until you're ready to eat.

TIP   The rotis will keep well in an airtight container for 2–3 days. To warm them up, pat them with damp kitchen paper and then either microwave for 30 seconds or heat them on a warm flat griddle or frying pan for 10 seconds on each side until hot.

CHUKANDAR KHEERE KA RAITA
COOLING BEETROOT AND CUCUMBER YOGHURT

SERVES 4
500g low-fat natural yoghurt
Pinch of salt
150g pickled beetroot
¼ cucumber
Small handful of dill, chopped
1 tsp cumin seeds
3 pinches of chilli powder
2 pinches of black salt

Pretty in pink, this gently spiced and soothing yoghurt provides a feast of colour and a robust antidote to spicy food. I barely remember a meal in my childhood without raita, thanks to the dairy-loving north Indian side of my family.

This recipe uses ready-pickled beetroot to save time and effort – the grated packs in supermarkets do nicely and will save your fingers from the inevitable pink stains. If you have pomegranate seeds, scatter them over as garnish. And if you don't have black salt, you could use Himalayan pink salt or sea salt.

Prepare the yoghurt by loosening it with 2 tablespoons of cold water in a shallow bowl or serving dish. Add the pinch of salt.

Grate the beetroot and cucumber (unless your pickled beetroot is ready-grated) and stir them both into the yoghurt. If you want a patterned effect rather than a vibrant pink, just swirl the beetroot instead of mixing it through fully. Stir half the dill through the raita, reserving the rest to garnish.

Place the raita in the fridge while you prepare your garnish. Toast the cumin seeds in a small pan for 20 seconds over a medium heat until fragrant and warm. Then tip into a pestle and mortar and crush finely.

Dust the ground cumin over your raita, along with the chilli powder and black salt. Sprinkle over the remaining dill and serve chilled.

VARIATIONS ⟩ CHANA RAITA
Instead of beetroot, cucumber and dill, add a 400g tin of rinsed and drained chickpeas to the yoghurt and a handful each of chopped mint and coriander leaves.

⟩ KACHUMBAR RAITA
Chop 1 large tomato, ¼ cucumber and 1 small onion into small pieces and stir into the yoghurt without adding any water to loosen it. Chop a small handful of coriander, stir half of it through the raita and scatter the other half over the top.

DRINKS

WHATEVER THE WEATHER OR OCCASION, INDIANS WILL RAISE A GLASS TO IT.

Come hot weather, we have plenty of cooling drinks that are designed to bring the temperature down: jugs of rose-flavoured Gulab Sharbat are habitually parked in the fridge at the very first sign of heat. In winter or on rainy days, warm Chai comes to the rescue.

Even to this day, every ailment, emotion or feeling has an instant antidote in form of a drink, if my family is to be believed. For everything else, there is always alcohol...

This chapter salutes the beverages of the nation – some old, some new and all irresistible. Ice-cold sweet Lassi provides cold comfort on hot days, while savoury Borhani and sweet Thandai make a fragrant appearance on festive days to cool and comfort, proving that spices aren't just for curries.

There are, of course, some not so traditional brews in this chapter. My love of a Bellini combines with chilli-spiked lychees to make a great aperitif (according to guests, at any rate). Rose syrup (*rooh afza*), the classic summer drink of the nation, makes an appearance not only in a lassi but also as a mixer for the tonic I always have in the fridge for a well-deserved G&T!

So add a dash of the exotic – at dinner parties, informal drinks or simply with brunch or snacks – and enjoy your next Indian meal with one of the drinks in the pages that follow.

GULAB SHARBAT

MUDDLED MINT, ROSE AND LEMON COOLER

MAKES 4 SMALL GLASSES
2 lemons, halved
8–10 mint leaves
5–6 tbsp Indian rose syrup
Ice
300ml soda water or water

The taste of summer in a glass, fresh lemon and mint is muddled together and then poured into tall glasses with Indian rose syrup or *rooh afza*. This deep pink cordial is made with a secret blend of floral essences and citric acid.

Sharbat usually has a tooth-tingling sweetness; in this cooler, I have saved your teeth somewhat. You can also try it with tonic water, if you fancy a change. Keep the sharbat chilled in the fridge to welcome guests on hot days.

Place the halved lemons in a glass jug or jar with the mint leaves. With the bottom of a thick rolling pin or wooden spoon, press down on the lemons to extract their juice and fragrant oils from the zest.

Now add the rose syrup and leave this to sit covered in the fridge until you're ready to serve.

To serve, strain equal quantities into four glasses filled with ice. Top with soda water or water and stir carefully.

LYCHEE CHILLI BELLINI

SERVES 4
4 green chillies, plus 4 to decorate
(optional)
6–10 lychees, peeled and stoned
if fresh
Prosecco or Cava

Spicy green chillies steeped in blended lychees offer a tropical twist to the classic Italian Bellini. When lychees are in season these juicy, translucent fruit are guaranteed to drip down your chin as you bite into them. While I am a great lover of a Bellini, I did draft in the services of friend and cocktail connoisseur Linda to make sure I was getting this right.

This is not a recipe so much as a method, as you can do whatever you like, as long as you are sober while doing it. If fresh lychees are not available, go for the tinned ones in light syrup. Tilt the flutes and pour the drink in gently as it's prone to bubbling over.

Deseed one of the chillies and blend it with the lychees in a hand blender to make a thick purée. Pour into a bowl.

Slit 3 of the remaining chillies lengthways, keeping the tops intact, and steep in the purée, gently pressing them against the sides of the bowl to get their heat going. Leave this in the fridge to chill for a couple of hours.

When you are ready to serve, spoon equal amounts of the purée into four champagne flutes, drop a whole chilli into each glass, if you want, and top with your chosen bubbles.

BORHANI

MINTY DIGESTIVE DRINKING YOGHURT

SERVES 4

8 mint sprigs

8 coriander sprigs

4 tsp cumin seeds

500g low-fat natural yoghurt

4 garlic cloves

8 whole black peppercorns

2 green chillies

Black salt or sea salt

A mint green drink, Borhani is traditionally served as a cooling accompaniment to biryani in Calcutta and Bangladesh, where the layered rice dish is filled with rich ghee, heady floral essences and warming spices. It makes an appearance especially during weddings and Eid, where biryani is one of several heavy meat-based centrepieces.

Consider Borhani a drinking raita, with a fragrant and floral taste explosion of its own despite the cooling effect of the yoghurt. Serve with Gosht Biryani (page 83) or alongside a full Indian meal.

Strip the mint leaves off their stalks to avoid a bitter aftertaste and chop the bottom ends off the coriander stalks and discard.

In a small frying pan, dry-roast the cumin seeds for 10 seconds over a medium heat until warm and fragrant. Toss the seeds into a smoothie maker or high-speed blender along with the yoghurt, garlic, black peppercorns, green chillies, mint leaves and coriander.

Blend until smooth, adding salt to taste, then pour into glasses and chill until you're ready to drink.

GULABI LASSI
STRAWBERRY AND ROSE SMOOTHIE

SERVES 4

12 medium ripe strawberries
12 green cardamom pods
800g natural yoghurt
250ml (1 cup) whole milk
4 tbsp Indian rose syrup
4–6 tbsp sugar, or to taste

This refreshing and creamy smooth drink from dairy-loving Punjab combines the very best of British and Indian summers. Rose syrup, poured into glasses filled with ice and water is a hot weather must from my Indian childhood, where strawberries have since become popular. Together they shine in lassi, described quite aptly as the 'air conditioner of Punjab'!

You can replace the strawberries with any fruit purée as long as it isn't acidic — mango would be a good choice. Chill well before you drink your Lassi and enjoy it with brunch alongside butter-topped Aloo Parathas (page 106) like a good Punjabi, or as a teatime cooler or sweet after-dinner digestif. *Recipe and variations pictured overleaf.*

Wash and hull the strawberries.

Lightly bash the whole cardamom pods in a pestle and mortar to remove the seeds. Discard the husks and toss the seeds into a smoothie maker or high-speed blender along with the strawberries, yoghurt, milk and rose syrup. Blitz until smooth.

Add the sugar — just 2 tablespoons to begin with, then taste and adjust to your liking.

VARIATIONS

> PAPAYA AND TOASTED FENNEL
> Dry-roast 2 teaspoons of fennel seeds in a small frying pan for 30 seconds. Deseed and peel 4 small or 2 large ripe papayas. Replace the strawberries and rose syrup with the toasted fennel and papaya and blend with the cardamom seeds, yoghurt and milk, adding sugar to taste.

> NUTELLA AND PEANUT BUTTER
> Replace the strawberries and rose syrup with 8 tablespoons each of Nutella and peanut butter, and 4 tablespoons of cocoa powder. Blend until smooth with the cardamom seeds, yoghurt and milk, adding sugar to taste.

MASALA CHAI
ULTIMATE SPICED TEA

SERVES 4

250ml (1 cup) whole milk
2.5cm fresh root ginger, finely grated
6 green cardamom pods
5cm cinnamon stick
4 small or 2 large bay leaves
4 standard tea bags
6 tsp sugar

Fragrant, warming and sweet, masala chai is the ultimate Indian cuppa. While the British introduced regular tea drinking to India, we couldn't resist turning it into our own spiced concoction. At railway stations, a glass or cup is hard to resist as the cries of *chai chai chai garam* (literally: 'tea tea tea hot') pierce the air.

In home kitchens, Masala Chai is made to order. Aromatic whole spices are freshly brewed with grated ginger. Whole milk is important, as the volatile oils from the spices need the fat in the dairy to release their full flavour. The method here is from my brother-in-law, who made cups of Masala Chai for us to wake up to while on holiday in Europe. If enjoying it at teatime, consider having some snacks like Pakoras (page 118) or Masala Vada (page 122) to nibble on.

Pour 1 litre (4 cups) cold water and the milk into a large pan and add the ginger. Bash the cardamom pods in a pestle and mortar and toss whole into the pan along with the cinnamon stick and bay leaves.

Bring the spiced milk to a rapid boil over a high heat. When it starts bubbling, submerge the tea bags and boil for a minute. If the milk looks like it's going to bubble over, just lower the heat or take the pan off the heat briefly. Then switch the heat off, cover and leave to sit for 2–2½ minutes, depending on how strong you like your cuppa. In the meantime, get your strainer and cups ready.

Strain into four cups, stir 1½ teaspoons of sugar into each cup and enjoy hot. You didn't hear this from me but if your tea goes cold, you can reheat and drink it.

VARIATIONS

> ADRAKWALI CHAI
> Turn this into gingered tea by brewing it with just the cardamom pods and 5cm fresh root ginger.

> KADAK MASALA CHAI
> Make a strong cuppa for bitterly cold days by adding a pinch each of whole black peppercorns and cloves and 1 star anise.

THANDAI

FENNEL, PISTACHIO AND MILK SHERBET

MAKES 4 TALL OR 8 SMALL DRINKS

1 tbsp blanched almonds

1 tbsp raw pistachios

3 tbsp poppy seeds

1 tbsp sunflower seeds

1½ tbsp fennel seeds

½ tsp freshly ground black pepper

1.2 litres (4½ cups) whole milk

10 green cardamom pods

4 tbsp rose water

5 tbsp sugar

Saffron threads and dried
    rose petals, to decorate

Thandai is a richly spiced milk drink thickened with almonds, pistachios and poppy and sunflower seeds. Meaning 'cooling drink', it is hugely popular at Holi, the Hindu Festival of Colours, decorated with saffron and dried rose petals. Gin and vodka also feature in cocktail versions of this drink at parties (see the variation below).

While normally you would use melon seeds in this drink, sunflower seeds are easier to source. Should you, like yours truly, happen to purchase a salted version of said seeds by accident or due to lack of choice, simply rinse them well before soaking.

Add the almonds, pistachios, poppy seeds, sunflower seeds, fennel seeds and black pepper to 250ml (1 cup) of the milk and place in the fridge to soak for 3–4 hours.

Lightly bash the cardamom pods to remove the seeds; discard the husks.

Add the soaked nuts and seeds with the soaking milk to a smoothie maker or high-speed blender along with the rose water, cardamom seeds, remaining milk and sugar. Blitz until smooth.

Strain the drink through a sieve to get any errant large bits of spice out of the way. Pour into four tumblers or eight cocktail glasses and chill until ice-cold. Decorate with saffron threads and rose petals before serving.

VARIATION ➤ For a boozy Thandai, add 2 measures of either vodka or gin into the tumblers or 1 measure into the small glasses. Stir well before decorating.

BADAM DOODH
ALMOND, SAFFRON AND TURMERIC MILK

SERVES 2–4

4 handfuls of blanched almonds

1 litre (4 cups) almond milk

1 tsp ground turmeric

Pinch of freshly ground black pepper

Sugar, to taste

4 pinches of saffron threads,
    plus extra to decorate

This warm mug of almond milk spiced with aphrodisiac saffron is a wedding night special. Traditionally, Hindu marriages are arranged, which means the bride and groom barely know each other before the wedding; they are then expected to consummate the relationship after a week-long celebration. Badam Doodh delivers a shot of energy to the exhausted couple, protein for the libido, a bit of calm for wedding night jitters and much entertainment for tittering relatives.

The 'superfood' turmeric is also sometimes added, and I have used it in my recipe, which also happens to be dairy-free. The tiny bit of pepper, while not typical, aids the absorption of the turmeric. Don't wait for a special occasion to brew this warm mug of comfort.

Soak the almonds in the milk for 3–4 hours in the fridge and then blitz in a smoothie maker or high-speed blender.

Strain into a heavy-based pan and bring it to a gentle rolling boil over a low-medium heat. Stir through the turmeric and pepper and cook for a couple of minutes until the turmeric dissolves and the milk thickens.

Pour the milk into mugs and add sugar to your taste. Stir a pinch of saffron into each mug, leaving the drink to infuse while cooling down slightly. Decorate with more saffron threads and serve warm. You can also chill this for a refreshing summer cooler.

SWEET
TREATS

TIME NOW TO 'MOO MITHA KARO' OR SWEETEN YOUR MOUTH.

In India it is traditional to do this to complete a full meal, mark a special occasion or accept your host's gracious hospitality – even if you don't actually sit down to a meal in their home. Sweets are not just desserts and can be enjoyed at all times of the day, and liberally during festive celebrations. While I may have had a wary relationship with food as a child, I always launched into desserts with gusto.

In India, when we say sweet we mean business. Sweets or *mithai* are dripping in sugar, usually made by *mithaiwalas*. There is logic in the existence of professional sweetmakers in our culture. It is an art and a science, usually involving copious amounts of sugar, ghee and dairy. In fact, sugar and ghee are important auspicious offerings to Hindu gods during ceremonial prayers. However, you can always adjust the sugar levels to your personal taste and preference.

The recipes that follow bring a small but very satisfying end to a spice fest, Amrakhand, Phirni and Rasmalai among them. These small individual portions can be brought out in the event of post-dinner food coma or stowed away for your own personal satisfaction for days to come. If it's just a little hit of sugar you're after, the recipes for Katli, Laddoo and Namak Chocolate Peda are just the ticket and will also make excellent food gifts.

So sweeten you mouth and your life with these satisfying little treats, which you can enjoy with or without company.

AMRAKHAND
STRAINED MANGO YOGHURT

SERVES 4
500g Greek-style yoghurt
450g mango pulp
5 green cardamom pods
1 tbsp whole milk
½ tsp saffron threads
4 tbsp icing sugar
Pistachios, almonds or charoli,
    to serve

Creamy yoghurt, strained until it loses all its whey, then spiced, sweetened and chilled, this is the ultimate palate cooler from Gujarat and Maharashtra. This popular mango version is often served on special occasions with flatbreads or puris.

Mango pulp is conveniently available in a tin, whatever the season. If you do have fresh mangoes, simply purée the fruit to a thick pulp – 2–3 large mangoes should give you enough for this recipe. Serve with a smattering of nuts – charoli (small, nutty and almond-flavoured) are traditional but almonds and pistachios work well too.

Place the yoghurt and mango pulp in the middle of a fine tea towel or clean muslin cloth. Then lift up the edges and leave to hang tied from a tap or kitchen cupboard door, with a bowl underneath to catch the dripping liquid. As you're starting with thick yoghurt, this should take 2–4 hours. You know it's ready when you gently squeeze the top of the parcel and only little drips of whey escape the muslin.

Lightly bash the cardamom pods with a rolling pin to remove the seeds. Discard the husks and grind the seeds to a fine powder in a pestle and mortar. Warm the milk gently in a small pan, turn the heat off and add the saffron to infuse.

Tip the thick yoghurt and mango mixture into a bowl. Next mix the crushed cardamom, reserving a pinch or two, into the yoghurt, along with the sugar and saffron-infused milk. Taste the mixture to make sure it is not too tart, adding more sugar if needed.

Finally, spoon into glasses or bowls and chill. Serve with a dusting of ground cardamom and whatever nuts you have opted for.

VARIATIONS > SHRIKHAND
To make Shrikhand, simply leave the mango pulp out.

> STRAWBERRY SHRIKHAND
For a Strawberry Shrikhand, use 20 medium puréed strawberries, instead of the mango pulp.

MANGO KULFI
CARDAMOM AND SAFFRON ICE CREAM

MAKES 4–6
4 green cardamom pods
2 pinches of saffron threads
150ml (½ cup) evaporated milk
160ml (½ cup) condensed milk
2 large mangoes, peeled, stoned and
    puréed in a food processor (or use
    400g tinned mango pulp)
250ml (1 cup) double cream

Kulfi combines the creamy decadence of ice cream with the texture and appeal of an ice lolly. Come April, crates of Alphonso mangoes are a must-source from Indian shops to make this, as they are far sweeter than Kesar mangoes. Kesar mango pulp is available tinned, however, when mangoes are entirely out of season.

Traditionally, Kulfi involves the slow reduction of whole milk to create the caramel base. I can think of a million better things to do with my life than slowly stir milk so my method is a no-cook version using evaporated milk, condensed milk and double cream. Don't bother with kulfi moulds, as they can be tricky little devils. Look out for conical ice lolly moulds and plunge wooden lolly sticks into them as they are setting.

Crush the cardamom pods roughly to extract the seeds; discard the husks. Grind the seeds to a fine powder in a pestle and mortar, then add them to a bowl with the saffron, evaporated and condensed milks and mango pulp. Whisk until well combined. Gently stir in the double cream so it's mixed through but not whipped.

Pour the mix into your moulds and freeze for 2–3 hours until you can insert a lolly stick that stays upright. When the kulfi is frozen solid, in about 5–6 hours, warm the sides of the moulds either with your hands or by carefully dipping in warm water, before tipping out and enjoying.

VARIATIONS ❯ PISTACHIO AND ROSE KULFI
Dry-roast 75g raw shelled pistachios for a minute in a medium-hot pan. Use this instead of the mango pulp, along with 3 tablespoons of Indian rose syrup or 1½ tablespoons of rose water.

❯ COFFEE AND WALNUT KULFI
Mix 3 tablespoons of instant coffee granules with 4 tablespoons of hot water to make a paste. Blend this into the milk and cream mixture, along with 120g raw walnuts, instead of the mango.

RASMALAI

RICOTTA DUMPLINGS IN SAFFRON CREAM

SERVES 6

250g ricotta

3 tbsp milk powder (see page 206)

1 tbsp plain flour

4 tbsp golden caster sugar

4 green cardamom pods

1 × 410g tin evaporated milk

100ml whole milk

Pinch of saffron threads, plus extra
    to serve

10 raw shelled pistachios

These soft dumplings are traditionally made with homemade paneer, cooked in sugar syrup and then steeped slowly in evaporated milk infused with cardamom and saffron. Literally translating as cream (*malai*) in juice (*ras*), Rasmalai unsurprisingly has its origins in sweet-loving Bengal.

This version is a quickie that takes under half an hour and uses a handy tub of ricotta and whole milk powder. Leftovers will be lovely straight out of the fridge for at least a week.

Pre-heat the oven to 180°C/Fan 160°C/Gas 4 and line a baking sheet with baking parchment.

Tip the ricotta into a sieve to drain off any excess moisture, then put into a bowl. Add the milk powder, flour and 3 tablespoons of the sugar and mix together until smooth.

Now, fill a spring-loaded ice cream scoop and drop even mounds of the ricotta mix onto the baking sheet at regular intervals. When you have used up all the batter, bake in the oven for 20 minutes.

While that's cooking, lightly bash the cardamom pods to extract the seeds, then discard the husks and finely grind the seeds in a pestle and mortar.

Put the evaporated milk, whole milk and saffron threads into a heavy-based pan and gently warm over a medium heat. Whisk regularly, tipping half the ground cardamom into the milk, and then toss the pistachios into the mortar with the remaining cardamom and crush them roughly for later. Remove the milk from the heat when it starts bubbling.

When the dumplings are cooked place them in small bowls – one or two per person – then pour the saffron cream on top to come halfway up the dumplings. Serve hot, or after the rasmalai cools down slightly, sprinkling the crushed cardamom and pistachio mix on top.

PHIRNI
VANILLA CUSTARD

SERVES 4

4 green cardamom pods

50g rice flour

600ml chilled whole milk

2.5cm vanilla pod or ½ tsp vanilla
extract

2 pinches of saffron threads

3–4 tbsp caster sugar

12 raw shelled pistachios, crushed,
to decorate

This fragrant custard is creamy and smooth and is traditionally served in shallow clay bowls, giving the dessert a subtle earthiness. Dating back to the Mughal Empire and with roots in Persia, Phirni makes a welcome soothing end to the extravagant spread at Muslim weddings and at Eid.

Phirni also doubles up as a quick dessert or teatime pudding for unexpected visitors. Top it with fruit as suggested in the variations below to make it even more delectable.

Lightly bash the cardamom pods to extract the seeds. Discard the husks, then grind the seeds to a fine powder in a pestle and mortar.

Put the rice flour into a bowl, add 200ml of the milk and stir to make a smooth paste.

Put the remaining milk into a heavy-based pan with the vanilla pod or extract and bring to the boil over a medium-high heat. Use a whisk to keep stirring. When the milk starts bubbling, lower the heat to a simmer and stir in the flour and milk paste, the saffron and the sugar to taste. Use your whisk to stir the mixture. You want the rice flour to cook slowly, without burning the milk. In about 5–7 minutes you will see the mixture thickening to a custard that coats the whisk.

Now, turn the heat off, stir in the ground cardamom and pour into four little bowls (if you used a vanilla pod, remove it now). Let the phirni cool slightly then pop into the fridge to set completely. Top with the crushed pistachios before serving.

VARIATIONS ➤ BERRY PHIRNI
Top with seasonal berries, as well as the crushed pistachios.

➤ MANGO AND LYCHEE PHIRNI
Top with some mango and lychees, chopped into small pieces, as well as the crushed pistachios.

KHUBANI KA MEETHA
GINGERED APRICOT COMPOTE

SERVES 4

200g soft dried apricots
8 tbsp light brown or demerara sugar
2 star anise
2.5cm fresh root ginger, finely grated
4 pinches of saffron threads,
    plus extra to decorate
1 tbsp warm milk
300g crème fraîche
Crushed blanched almonds,
    to decorate

A Hyderabadi speciality, Khubani Ka Meetha is a masterstroke in simplicity when it comes to desserts – slow-cooked dried apricot compote with a touch of saffron, served with little more than thick cream. We owe our love of apricots to Babur, founder of the Mughal Dynasty in India, who popularised the use of the expensive fruit in regal desserts.

My recipe commits a terrible crime that is likely to annoy every aunty I met during my incredible travels in Hyderabad – the rogue addition of ginger. But it does pair really well with the sweet apricots. And the crème fraîche makes for a lighter touch than cream here.

Soak the apricots in 2 litres (8 cups) cold water for 2 hours in a medium pan. When the time is up, add the sugar and star anise to the water, place over a medium heat and bubble at a gentle simmer for 30 minutes. Keep an eye on the apricots throughout; you want the sugar to caramelise and a thick dark syrup to form around them.

After 30 minutes, mix in the grated ginger and cook for another 15 minutes. Meanwhile, steep the saffron in the warm milk.

Stab the apricots with a wooden spoon to break them up a bit when they are soft and pulpy. When there is no runny liquid in the pan, turn the heat off and leave the compote to cool.

Next, stir the saffron milk into the crème fraîche. Spoon this into four little serving dishes and then divide the cool compote between the dishes. Chill well before decorating with some crushed blanched almonds and a saffron thread or two.

NAMAK CHOCOLATE PEDA
SEA SALT AND COCOA MILK FUDGE

MAKES 8

8 green cardamom pods
50g golden caster sugar
125g (1 cup) milk powder
120g unsweetened cocoa powder
2 tbsp ghee
8 raw shelled pistachios
Sea salt flakes

Peda, pronounced *pay-rha*, is moist milk fudge subtly laced with ghee. Combined with dark cocoa and topped with sea salt, it makes a grown-up sweet that's not just for Diwali. It's amazing with cinnamon ice cream.

You can make Peda with condensed milk, but milk powder gives it its characteristic bite. The milk powder isn't infant formula – look for creamy whole milk versions among popular Indian brands like Natco or Fudco, both at Indian grocery stores and online. As for the cocoa, use the best quality Fair Trade version you can find.

Lightly bash the cardamom pods to extract the seeds, then discard the husks and grind the seeds to a powder in a pestle and mortar.

Put 125ml (½ cup) cold water and the sugar into a heavy-based pan. Bubble this, stirring regularly, over a medium heat for 5 minutes until it reduces in volume by half.

When the syrup is ready, lower the heat to a simmer and stir in the milk powder, cocoa and ground cardamom. Increase the heat to medium again and cook for another 5 minutes, stirring briskly to get rid of any lumps and make sure the mixture doesn't stick to the pan and burn. The mix will now look like a molten dough that doesn't spread easily in the warm pan.

Remove from the heat and tip the dough onto a plate lined with baking parchment. Let it cool for about 10–15 minutes until still molten but easy to handle. Smear ½ tablespoon of ghee in your palms, take a small ping-pong ball-sized amount of the dough and roll until smooth, then place on a plate. Use your thumb to make an imprint on the top, pressing the mound into a disc. Repeat with the remaining mixture, greasing your palms with more ghee as needed.

When you have eight discs, crush the pistachios in the pestle and mortar and use to fill the thumb indents in each one, then top with a tiny pinch of sea salt flakes. Chill until solid, store in an airtight container and enjoy for up to a week.

NARIYAL GAJAR HALWA LADDOO
COCONUT AND CARROT TRUFFLES

MAKES 12–16
4 green cardamom pods
1 tbsp ghee
4 medium carrots (about 450g), grated
125g (1¼ cups) desiccated coconut
1 × 400ml tin condensed milk
2 tbsp ground almonds

Laddoo, or *laddu*, are little balls of densely packed sweets that are rolled in ghee. They are reportedly the favourite sweet of elephant-headed god Lord Ganesh, and many extravagant versions have been developed by Indian sweet makers for his birthday celebration Ganesh Chaturthi. *Gajar* or carrot halwa is a classic north Indian pudding, in which carrots are cooked painstakingly in milk, ghee and sugar.

My recipe was born as a result of a carrot glut in my kitchen and uses handy shortcuts. If rolling truffles isn't your thing, simply spoon the dough into little bowls and sprinkle crushed skinned almonds and desiccated coconut on top to serve. It's lovely served warm with vanilla ice cream too.

Lightly crush the cardamom pods to remove the seeds, discarding the husks. Grind the seeds to a fine powder in a pestle and mortar.

Put the ghee into a heavy-based pan and place over a medium heat. When it's warm, add the grated carrots and cook them for 8–10 minutes until they are soft with little moisture left in them.

Add 100g (1 cup) of the coconut and the condensed milk and mix together for another 5–7 minutes until you get sticky dough that doesn't spread when you pull it towards a corner of the pan. Sprinkle in the ground cardamom and stir to combine. Remove from the heat.

Cover a plate with the ground almonds and the remaining desiccated coconut. Take walnut-sized pieces of the warm dough and roll them until round in the mix, then set on a plate and leave to cool.

These will last for 3–4 days in the fridge.

MEWA LADDOO
DATE AND NUT BALLS

MAKES 12–16
Handful of raw pistachios
Handful of raw cashews
Handful of raw blanched almonds
2 green cardamom pods
24 Deglet Noor dates, pitted
1 tbsp ghee
Sesame seeds or desiccated coconut,
    for rolling

Taking just minutes to make, dried fruit Laddoos are a handy snack for the sweet-toothed, and double up as great gifts. I buy giant sacks of pistachios, cashews and almonds from an ethnic store just before the Hindu Festival of Lights, Diwali, then make these and pack them up like truffles for gifting. Place the Laddoos in mini cupcake cases if you're serving to guests.

Toss the nuts into a dry pan set over a medium heat, along with the cardamom pods. Toast for 3–5 minutes until warm. Tip the lot into a food processor and crush roughly (if cardamom husks are objectionable to you, you could bash the pods to release the seeds and discard the husks before crushing). You want a coarse texture with no chunks of nut.

Now, roughly chop the dates, add them to a small pan with the ghee and soften them over a medium heat for a minute or two. You can also do this in the microwave. Warming the dates helps you blend and shape the laddoos later.

Add the ghee-covered dates to the nuts in the food processor and blend until the coarse mixture just comes together as a dough. Be wary of over-processing, as it will make it harder to roll them later.

Use a tablespoon or small ice cream scoop to take equal portions out of the bowl and roll into little balls on a plate dusted with the sesame seeds or desiccated coconut. Store in an airtight container and enjoy for up to a week.

KATLI
GHEE-LACED ALMOND MARZIPAN BITES

MAKES 16–20

4 green cardamom pods
200g (1 cup) white caster sugar
150g (1½ cups) ground almonds
2 tbsp ghee
16–20 edible silver leaf sheets,
    to decorate (optional)

Katli (pronounced *cut-li*) is a cross between marzipan and fudge, which invariably makes an appearance at Diwali, covered with edible silver leaves on decorated platters and gifted as part of the celebrations.

The secret to getting Katli right is making sugar syrup: the foolproof method is to bubble sugary water until just before it forms a string consistency. This keeps it moist and soft, which is the texture we're gunning for. Cut the Katli while it's still warm, as it will set quickly when cool.

Lightly bash the cardamom pods with a rolling pin to remove the seeds and then grind them to a fine powder in a pestle and mortar.

Pour 180ml (¾ cup) cold water into a medium pan, add the sugar and place over a high heat. When you see bubbles appearing in the pan, lower the heat to medium and keep it bubbling for 10 minutes. It will turn into a thick syrup (about half the volume) and you will see sugar crystals beginning to settle on the sides of the pan.

Add the cardamom, ground almonds and ghee and stir well for a minute to combine, until the mix doesn't spread when you pull it to one side.

Now tip the fudge onto a sheet of baking parchment and let it cool slightly until it's no longer sticky to the touch. Smooth with a rolling pin to a thickness of about 5mm. Then, while it's still warm, use a sharp knife to cut the fudge into diamonds. Leave to cool completely.

If you want to embellish your Katli with silver leaf, use a damp pastry brush to gently drape the leaves over and adhere them to the surface.

These will last for up to 2 weeks in an airtight container – if you don't snaffle them up within hours.

VARIATION ➤ You can use 1½ cups raw shelled pistachios or raw cashews instead of the ground almonds. Grind the nut of your choice in a small hand blender for 5 seconds in two batches. It's important to keep the grinder going without interruption for each batch and to not overdo it or the nuts will release their oils and turn into paste.

CHUTNEYS, PICKLES AND MORE

THERE IS NOTHING THAT WILL IMPRESS AN ELDERLY INDIAN MORE THAN HOMEMADE 'EXTRAS'.

My great aunt Lajjo Bua used to gift us a portion of her household pickle stash every winter, as we never made our own. And my mother took great joy in reminding me of the fresh cow's milk from our farm that she pasteurised and then creamed to make proper ghee when we were little. The standards are high in my family.

I am firmly of the 'shop-bought' school of thinking, as even in India pickles, papad and paneer are increasingly bought rather than made at home. However, this chapter goes gently retro on you. It contains added extras that you can choose to make at home if you have the time and inclination.

There is a guide to making ghee without a cowshed close by, paneer that will set without pain and an effortless garam masala. There are two recipes for pickle – one that is perfect for gifting to chilli-heads and another from my family that neither love nor money can buy.

There are chutneys you can make ahead and freeze, like Hara Chutney, a classic marriage of coriander, mint, chilli and lemon, as well as Coconut Chutney, the best accompaniment to the Dosa and Pesarattu in this book (pages 110 and 100). There are also two essentials for the busy, modern kitchen – a tomato curry paste that you can make and store for future use, and a trio of zero-effort instant chutneys.

So when life gives you lemons, make lemon pickle. For everything else, the following pages will liven up your meals and your life.

HARA CHUTNEY
GREEN CORIANDER, MINT AND CHILLI CHUTNEY

MAKES ENOUGH FOR 4–6
100g bunch of coriander
50g bunch of mint
Juice of 2–3 lemons
2 tsp sugar
2–4 green chillies
2 garlic cloves
1 tsp cumin seeds
½ tsp salt, or to taste

This spicy and sharp green chutney from north India is the perfect dipping sauce for Indian snacks and pancakes. In my family home, we always have a freshly made pot of this on the table, alongside jars of pickle. And it's not just for dipping – top baked fish fillets with it, slather it on cucumber sandwiches and use it as a salad dressing.

This recipe can be tweaked to your heart's content. Add more mint leaves, make it spicier with additional chillies and blend with a couple of tablespoons of Greek yoghurt to get a more muted, restaurant-style finish. Taste as you go along to get it just the way you like it. It keeps for up to a week in the fridge, or you can freeze it in ice-cube trays as a handy stash to defrost and use another day. *Recipe pictured on page 220.*

Wash the coriander and mint. Pick the mint leaves and discard the bitter stalks. Chop the coriander leaves, discarding the stalks.

Place the coriander and mint with the lemon juice, sugar, green chillies, garlic and cumin seeds in a small hand blender and purée until smooth. Add salt to make this as punchy as you can handle.

KHEJUR AAR TAMATAR CHATNI
TOMATO, DATE AND GINGER CHUTNEY

MAKES 2 × 250G JARS
600g ripe tomatoes
2 tsp mustard oil
1 tsp Bengali five-spice (panch phoron)
2.5cm fresh root ginger
2 tbsp light brown muscovado
    or palm sugar
1 whole dried red chilli
80g pitted dates

Gingered tomato and dates join forces in this spicy chutney, which is a lovely relish at parties, as well as making a great gift. If you're lucky enough to enjoy a glut of home-grown tomatoes in summer, this chutney is a great way to use up your bounty. Try it on Namak Pare (page 136) or with Samosas (page 128).

Interestingly, the word 'chutney' doesn't imply preservation in India – see page 238 for more on this. As this is fresh chutney, with no vinegar, it will keep for up to a week in the fridge, so make a jar for yourself and one to give away. But something tells me it may be gone well before that.

If you're giving this away as a gift, you may want to sterilise the jar by washing it thoroughly and placing it in an oven pre-heated to 140°C/Fan 120°C/Gas 1 for about 5 minutes until no moisture remains. If the lid isn't plastic, this can go in too. If it is, then place it in only after you turn the oven off to help dry it off.

Wash, dry and slice each tomato into eight pieces.

Warm the oil in a medium pan over a high heat and when it's hot, add the five-spice mix. It will splutter so immediately add the tomatoes, stir through once, then cover and cook for 10 minutes until the tomatoes soften.

Next, take the lid off and stir in the ginger, sugar and red chilli. Cook over a medium-high heat for another 30–35 minutes until the chutney darkens and thickens to a jam-like consistency. Add the dates and cook for a further 5 minutes.

Allow to cool slightly before removing and discarding the ginger and whole red chilli, then transfer the chutney to your jars.

TIP   Peeled and deseeded marrow also works well, instead of the tomatoes.

COCONUT CHUTNEY

FOR THE CHUTNEY
100g desiccated coconut
250ml (1 cup) hot water
1 green chilli
1cm fresh root ginger
1 tsp tamarind paste
½ tsp salt, or to taste
2 tbsp split Bengal gram,
    dry-roasted in a pan (or use
    2 tbsp Greek-style yoghurt)

FOR THE TEMPERING
1 tbsp coconut oil
Pinch of asafoetida
2 pinches of split Bengal gram
    (optional)
½ tsp mustard seeds
2 whole dried red chillies,
    broken in half
10–15 curry leaves

Spicy, fragrant and an essential accompaniment to south India's fermented foods, coconut chutney is a must-have in every Indian kitchen. This is the most common south Indian chutney, but each state and family has its own variations. If I don't have split Bengal gram to hand, I often use Greek yoghurt to thicken the chutney instead. This can easily be whipped up on a quiet evening and, although it's borderline heretic, I confess I often forgo the tempering.

Use a small hand blender or high-speed blender to grind the coconut down well. Desiccated coconut beefed up with the coconut oil in the tempering does just fine, but use fresh coconut if you have it, adding less hot water to get the desired thick but smooth consistency. *Recipe pictured on page 111*.

First put the coconut into a blender, along with the hot water, and leave to sit for 5 minutes until it rehydrates.

Now, add the rest of the chutney ingredients to the blender and purée until creamy and integrated, but still with some texture. Check for salt and add more if you need to, blending again gently to mix it in. Now tip the chutney into a bowl and make the tempering.

Put the coconut oil into a small frying pan and place over a high heat. When it's hot, tip in the asafoetida and then add the rest of the ingredients in quick succession. As soon as the curry leaves sizzle up, pour the lot over the coconut chutney.

This will last in an airtight container for up to a week in the fridge or in the freezer for up to a month. Stir well before serving.

TIP   You can add an extra green chilli, 4 tablespoons of chopped coriander or both to the coconut before grinding into a paste, for a herby twist on the main recipe.

INSTACHUTNEYS
QUICK AND EASY CHUTNEY TRIO

MAKES ENOUGH FOR 4–6

1. MUSTARD
2 green chillies
2 tbsp French wholegrain mustard
2 tsp English mustard
2 tbsp mustard oil

2. TAMARIND AND PEANUT
1 tsp soft light brown sugar
1 tbsp hand-hot water
1 tsp tamarind paste
1 tbsp smooth peanut butter
   (with no added sugar or salt)

3. TOMATO CHILLI
3 tbsp tomato ketchup
3 drops extra-hot chilli sauce

Sharp, spiky and excellent for dunking, chutneys often complete a meal. Saying that, unless I am planning ahead and being exceptionally organised, chutneys are always the last things I get around to. Here's where cheat's chutneys, or what I call 'instachutneys', come in very handy. You can whip these up in no time and spend the extra moments gloating at your brilliance. *Recipes pictured overleaf.*

1. MUSTARD
Finely chop the green chillies, add them to a bowl with the rest of the ingredients and stir until combined.

2. TAMARIND AND PEANUT
Stir the sugar and warm water together in a bowl, then mix in the other ingredients.

3. TOMATO CHILLI
Stir the spiciest chilli sauce you have into ketchup for an instant tomato chilli sauce.

HARI MIRCHI KA ACHAR

EXPLOSIVE CHILLI AND MUSTARD PICKLE

MAKES 1 × 400–500ML JAR
50 green chillies (about 100g)
2 tsp black mustard seeds
2 tsp fenugreek seeds
3 tbsp mustard oil
¼ tsp asafoetida
1 tsp ground turmeric
1 tbsp sea salt
4 tbsp lemon juice

Indian pickles have a mouth-puckering, sense-exploding way about them – they are perfect condiments, whether served alongside a meal or simply slathered on toast. My family have been known to carry pots of their favourite pickle around holidays in Europe to escape the routine misery of delicately seasoned food.

Making pickle is something of a dying art in India, but many families still preserve this tradition. British spring sunshine provides the ideal temperature to kick-start the fermentation process of this particular pickle.

Wash the jar thoroughly and sterilise it by placing it in an oven pre-heated to 140°C/Fan 120°C/Gas 1 for about 5 minutes until no moisture remains. If the lid isn't plastic, this can go in too. If it is, then place it in only after you turn the oven off to help dry it off.

Let the jar cool while you wash and dry the green chillies. I wipe them dry with kitchen paper and then leave them on a clean tea towel to air.

Meanwhile, dry-roast the mustard and fenugreek seeds in a small frying pan over a medium heat for 30 seconds and then grind to a powder in a pestle and mortar or coffee grinder.

Next, warm the mustard oil and add the asafoetida and turmeric. When they sizzle, switch the heat off and leave to cool.

Slice the green chillies into 1cm-long pieces and put them into a clean, dry bowl. Add the sea salt, ground toasted spices and lemon juice. Mix thoroughly and spoon into the sterilised jar. Finish by pouring the cooled spicy oil all over the pickles in the jar. Seal the top of the jar with a layer of cling film and put the lid on top.

Place the jar on a sunny windowsill. Stir the pickle and gently push it under the oil with a clean, dry spoon once a day, replacing the cling film if needed. If the sun is missing, just bring it to a warm and dry place indoors. In 7–10 days your pickle should be ready – soft but with a bite. Place it in the fridge and enjoy it for months to come.

NIMBU KA ACHAR

SALTY SOUR PRESERVED LEMON PICKLE

MAKES 3 × 500G JARS
1kg unwaxed organic lemons
100g sea salt flakes
1 tbsp ground turmeric
1½ tsp chilli powder
1½ tsp homemade garam masala
    (page 227)
1½ tsp sugar (optional)

Tart and salty, this lemon pickle is a staple project in north Indian homes in crisp, sunny winters. In my all-time favourite *National Indian Association of Women Cookbook*, Debolina Mazumdar intriguingly claims, 'The pickle is served to invalids who crave a change in their menu and want pickels' *[sic]*. Debolina's recipe provided a starting point for my own recipe. I then called my grandma, whose Delhi family home is famous for its pickles. Nani is practically deaf, and we had an awkward conversation until she registered the words 'Nimbu Ka Achar' and burst into life.

I know this is a massive amount of lemons but believe me, you won't want to spend two months fermenting for just a tiny pot.

Wash the jars thoroughly and sterilise them (see opposite).

Now, wash and dry the lemons well. Cut them into half and then quarters, removing the pips, and put them into a large, clean glass bowl. Add the salt and turmeric to the bowl, mixing well to incorporate with the lemons. Spoon into the jars, tipping in any liquid that remains in the bowl.

Seal the top of each jar with a layer of cling film and then tightly close the lids. Put the jars on a sunny windowsill to ferment. You'll see the salt extracting the juices from the lemons and the brine rising to submerge the fruit. Stir this with a clean, dry spoon every day for 2 weeks, pushing the lemons down into the liquid and removing any pips that rise to the surface. Change the cling film occasionally and reseal.

After 2 weeks, the lemons will have softened and turned a paler shade. Now, stir equal amounts of the chilli powder, garam masala and sugar into each jar – you will only need to add the sugar if you taste the pickle and find it too tart. Move the pickle to a dark, warm spot and leave for another 6–8 weeks, stirring every other day.

Your pickle will be done when the lemons and their rinds are soft and dark. Store this in the fridge, where it will go on maturing and deepening in colour – according to my grandmother it will keep for up to 10 years!

DESI GHEE
INDIAN CLARIFIED BUTTER

MAKES 1 × 200ML JAR
600ml fresh double cream
120g organic live natural yoghurt
    (not low-fat)
Pinch of sea salt

The purest form of fat, ghee has a sublime smoky, warm and buttery quality that magically lifts recipes. Often referred to as 'liquid gold', ghee is lauded in Ayurveda, the ancient Hindu system of medicine, for its ability, in moderation, to balance all three body types or *doshas*. While ghee is often described as clarified butter, it really is clarified *cultured* butter. The fermentation part of this is important as it gives ghee the unique tangy taste that makes it so irresistible.

My mother used to squirrel away the cream from freshly pasteurised milk for up to 10 days before setting the cook on ghee-making duties. If, like me, you have no cows to milk, opt for shop-bought fresh cream instead.

Wash the jar thoroughly and sterilise it (see page 222).

Put the cream into a heavy-based wok and stir through the yoghurt. Leave this to sit loosely covered until it starts thickening, taking on colour and smelling slightly sour. If it's cold you can leave it on your worktop for anywhere between 8 and 24 hours. If it's extremely hot, stick this in the fridge for 2–3 days until you get the same result.

Bring the cultured cream to the boil over a medium-low heat, stirring regularly. If it starts spitting and hissing, you can loosely cover, using the cover as a shield to protect your clothes when stirring.

In about 10 minutes, you'll see ghee escaping from the cream. In another few minutes, the ghee will start frothing and the milk solids will turn into golden crumbs. When the froth covers the milk solids completely, remove from the heat and add the salt.

Carefully pass the ghee through a sieve into a measuring jug, pressing down the milk solids to extract as much of the liquid as possible. Tip the solids collected in the sieve into a bowl and continue until the wok is empty. Then line the open mouth of your jar with muslin and strain the ghee through it into the jar. (The leftover solids are delectable swirled into warm rice.)

Enjoy the ghee for months – as it's a pure form of fat there's no need to keep in the fridge (it will be solid at room temperature).

PANEER
HOMEMADE INDIAN CHEESE

MAKES ABOUT 300G
2.25 litres whole milk
80ml strained lemon juice

Paneer is readily available in shops, but this homemade version is easy enough to whip up. At its simplest it is whole milk brought to a boil, curdled with an acid – lemon juice, vinegar or yoghurt – and then strained. Just be careful when you stir homemade paneer into curry, as it is more delicate than its shop-bought counterpart.

Bring the milk to the boil over a medium-high heat in a heavy-based pan. Meanwhile, drape a muslin cloth over a large bowl and place a colander or sieve with a flat base securely over another bowl with lots of space underneath for drainage.

As you see the milk starting to boil, stir through the lemon juice. It will curdle but this is all good. Turn off the heat.

Carefully pour the curdled milk into the muslin. Lift the edges of the muslin and gently twist the top to drain off any excess whey. Now carry this over to the sink, holding the bowl under it to catch any drops, and wash under a cold tap, while holding the paneer securely inside the muslin. This not only washes the acidic smell off but also prevents the paneer from turning rubbery. Twist the muslin gently to squeeze out the excess dripping whey.

Loosen the muslin and spread the paneer out to an even depth in the base of your colander or sieve, while still in its parcel. Place a heavy-duty weight on top of the bundle – I can recommend a flat plate, then a heavy cookbook or two and a cast-iron pan.

Leave the paneer to drain and firm up for a couple of hours. When the time is up, cut or crumble and use within a couple of days. You can also submerge it in fresh water in an airtight container and keep it in the fridge for up to a week, changing the water daily. If you decide to fry it, pat dry before using or it will splutter relentlessly in the pan.

SPROUTED BENGAL GRAM

MAKES ABOUT 4 LARGE HANDFULS
200g whole Bengal gram

Germinating pulses until they are more nutritious, easily digestible and living versions of themselves is a much-loved tradition in India, and the resultant sprouts are lightly cooked or consumed raw. Typically, sprouted whole Bengal gram (brown chickpeas) are used raw in Jhalmuri (page 140) and Kala Chana Chaat (page 150). You can also toss them into savoury pancake batters, or add them to salads and smoothies.

Wash the whole Bengal gram well and soak them in a large bowl of fresh cold water overnight. The following day, drain and rinse them.

Line a colander with a muslin cloth or clean tea towel, tip the Bengal gram in and loosely pull the edges of the cloth over to cover. Set aside somewhere cool and spritz them with a little cold water every 6–8 hours, gently shaking them around to keep them evenly moist. You're allowed the odd impatient peek.

Your sprouts should be ready in 2–3 days, depending on how warm it is in your kitchen – ideally the seedlings should be at least 1cm long.

Wash the sprouts thoroughly and tip onto a few sheets of kitchen paper to dry out. When they are dry, store them in an airtight container in the fridge for up to 3–4 days.

GARAM MASALA
WARMING SPICE BLEND

MAKES 3 TABLESPOONS
4 green cardamom pods
2 black cardamom pods
1 tsp whole black peppercorns
¾ tsp cloves
2 medium bay leaves
2.5cm cinnamon stick

Translating literally as 'hot spice', Garam Masala is a warming blend of roasted and ground whole spices. It lifts a dish, balancing tangy, sweet and creamy flavours. Unless a recipe specifically says otherwise, sprinkle garam masala towards the end of cooking to reap its full benefit and to prevent the dish from going bitter. Ready-made is absolutely fine, but for special occasions you can't beat a batch of the fresh stuff.

In India the exact combination of whole spices that go into garam masala varies from home to home, and region to region. My version is a simple one but you can go wild and experiment by adding coriander, cumin, nutmeg, mace, fennel, star anise, ground ginger and even rose petals. Whatever you do, make a small quantity at a time and use it quickly to make the most of all that potent flavour.

Dry-roast the spices in a frying pan over a medium heat for 2 minutes until you can smell their fragrant aroma. Then turn the heat off and leave to cool.

Grind the cooled spices, including the cardamom husks, in a pestle and mortar or coffee grinder until you have a fine powder. Use immediately for full effect or transfer to an airtight jar and keep for up to 6 months.

TAMATAR MASALA
HOMEMADE FRESH TOMATO CURRY PASTE

MAKES 3 PORTIONS
6 tbsp oil
3 medium onions, thinly sliced
½ tsp salt
12 garlic cloves, finely grated
8cm fresh root ginger, finely grated
6 ripe medium tomatoes, diced
1½ tsp ground turmeric
1½ tsp chilli powder

Making fresh ingredient pastes that can subsequently be used in various guises is a shortcut loved by many of today's Indian home cooks. Tamatar Masala is my favourite – a portion of this makes a breeze of the numerous steps used to make the base of so many of our dishes: softening and caramelising onions, cooking ginger and garlic and helping spices go from raw and pungent to something altogether more aromatic and irresistible. Make this ahead of time and turn it into versatile meals as and when you crave an Indian spice kick. The trick is to keep the masala relatively simple, giving you a chance to tweak the recipe later by adding more spices or a bit of tamarind, for example.

Pour the oil into a large pan and place over a medium-high heat. When it's hot, toss in the sliced onions along with the salt and cook for 10 minutes. Add the garlic and ginger to the onions and cook for another 10 minutes. By this point the whole mixture should be turning golden. If it starts sticking to the bottom of the pan, add a couple of tablespoons of hot water and scrape loose.

Add the diced tomatoes along with the turmeric and chilli powder. Stir the mixture well for another 15 minutes until the tomatoes disintegrate and turn pulpy.

Finally, lower the heat to a high simmer, cover and cook for 5 minutes until you see oil oozing out of little pores on the surface of the masala.

Cool and store in three portions. The masala should last for up to 3–4 days in the fridge and up to 2 months in the freezer. Warm it up in a pan before continuing with your recipe. You can use it in any curry that starts with tomato and onion, or toss it into the Tadka Dal (page 172) or Khichdi (page 46).

INGREDIENTS

Indian cooking uses an often overwhelming array of ingredients, ranging from the exotic to the familiar. Those most commonly used are listed here for easy reference. Always refer to the product packaging, recipes and your instinct as a home cook for shelf life and quality.

AN INTRODUCTION TO SPICES

There are a vast number of spices used in Indian cooking, which can be daunting. Saying that, most Indian homes will stock a core range of spices that cover essential recipes with a few more exotic ones thrown in for good measure. I have listed the spices used in this book accordingly. All of them can be used in at least two recipes, if not more.

Shopping for Indian spices in London used to be an annual family ritual for us. We'd return from European summer holidays desperate for *ghar ka khana* (home-cooked Indian food) and dash to Drummond Street for spice shops and takeaway kebabs. I keep the time-honoured tradition alive by routinely terrorising the local Indian neighbourhood with my spirited children.

When I first started cooking, buying spices meant making special trips to the Indian spice shop or requesting our friendly neighbourhood newsagent to source them for me. Indian spices and ingredients have since become much more widely available in supermarkets and local shops, but if a trip to the shops isn't practical, there is always the internet. You can easily source fresh curry leaves online, for instance, or even a curry sapling to grow at home.

Importantly, you won't need every spice listed here all at once. Start building your collection around the recipes that titillate your taste buds the most and go from there.

Ready-ground spices are absolutely fine, unless the recipe calls for freshly roasted and ground. Traditionally these are stored in a *masala dabba*, a stainless steel tin with removable bowl inserts, but any airtight jar will do.

If you have the whole version of a spice, dry-roast it gently in a pan over a medium heat for 30 seconds to release its oils, then grind it in a pestle and mortar or spice grinder. A teaspoon of whole spice will yield roughly 1½ teaspoons when ground.

As a general rule, buy spices in small quantities unless you are planning to cook Indian food a lot. Ground spices, in particular, lose their potent flavour over time. (On the other hand, buy *big* bags of fresh herbs and wash, dry and freeze them for up to two months of use.) While having use-by dates on ingredients is useful, I support the old-school five senses approach to determine if they're past their best: look out for a change in colour, aroma, texture or taste and always trust your judgement.

The collection below features the spices that you can use in a large number of recipes in this book.

ASAFOETIDA   HING
This powdered member of the fennel family is deceptively foul-smelling; however, when sparingly sprinkled into hot oil it mimics buttery onion and garlic. A digestive aid, it is used in lentil, bean and meat dishes to magical effect. It's also known as Devil's Dung, so keep this spice tightly sealed in a jar so its aromas don't impregnate the entire contents of the cupboard!

BAY LEAVES   TEJ PATTA
The authentic bay leaf called for in Indian cooking has three veins and is actually a cinnamon leaf, as opposed to the Mediterranean bay leaf commonly used in Europe. The latter is milder, more lemony and smoky than *tej patta*. They also have just one leaf spine. My recipes are adjusted for the European version, as they're easier to get hold of and widely used overseas. If you find the Indian bay leaf, halve the amount of any cinnamon also used in the recipe.

CARDAMOM   ELAICHI
You can buy cardamom both as a small green pod and a large black one. While you can buy bags of cardamom seeds, they do lose their potent aroma quickly; I prefer to buy the whole pods and lightly crush them in a pestle and mortar to extract the seeds. The whole green *elaichi* is used to delicately flavour curries, while its seeds are ground and used

in desserts. The black *elaichi* is used as a powerful aromatic in curries and rice dishes, often sizzled whole in hot oil.

CINNAMON   DALCHINI
The cinnamon commonly used in Indian cooking is actually cassia bark and looks like the bark of a tree. I prefer Ceylon cinnamon, the kind that's rolled into bundles, as it has a more intense flavour and more health benefits, but you can use either. Cinnamon releases its aroma when sizzled in hot oil at the start of the recipe.

CLOVES   LAVANG
Robust in their anise notes, like cinnamon sticks, cloves are sizzled in hot oil at the beginning of a recipe to release their flavour into the oil. They are usually used sparingly and often in conjunction with cinnamon.

CORIANDER SEEDS   DHANIYA
These crunchy, hollow, dried out berries are used mostly in ground form, and are often employed to add bulk to shop-bought garam masala. Coriander seeds have a sharp bitter lemon edge – not to be confused with fresh coriander leaves!

CUMIN SEEDS   JEERA
A natural partner to coriander seeds, these are used whole or ground. They have a distinct smoky and warm flavour, released when the seeds are sizzled in hot oil or used in ground form. When dry-roasted and ground, cumin seeds intensify and turn earthier – great for adding a finishing touch to dishes. Bear in mind that they do burn quickly when being toasted or sizzled in oil.

DRIED FENUGREEK LEAVES   KASOORI METHI
Bitter and sharp, dehydrated fenugreek leaf is the rock star of Punjabi cooking. It lifts creamy curries and balances the tang in tomatoes, with an addictive flavour. You can crumble it over curries but I favour soaking a pinch in a little hot water and then stirring through towards the end of cooking.

FENNEL SEEDS SAUNF
Fennel seeds are pale green in colour and sport a similar zingy flavour to aniseed. They are often toasted and then chewed along with sugar crystals following a meal as a mouth freshener. Buy them whole or ground, depending on the recipe.

GARAM MASALA
This is a combination of earthy and dark whole spices, toasted until aromatic and then ground to a fine powder. It is perfectly acceptable to buy this ready-made, although the freshly ground version (page 227) is punchy and makes a great gift. It is usually added at the end of a recipe to inject dishes with aroma and warmth; if added too soon garam masala can turn a dish bitter, so do follow the recipe.

KASHMIRI CHILLIES DEGHI MIRCH
Because of their mildness, Kashmiri chillies are added mostly for the deep red hue they impart to dishes. I always have a jar of whole dried Kashmiri chillies and the ground version lying around, but you can also substitute the latter with one part chilli powder to three parts paprika.

MUSTARD SEEDS RAI
A must-have for cooking the food of south India and Gujarat, these are the seeds of the mustard plant. The black/brown mustard seeds are used widely in cooking, while the yellow/white varieties are deployed in pickling because of their preservative qualities. Watch out for popping seeds trying to escape the hot oil when frying.

SAFFRON ZAFRAN
Fragrant and reassuringly expensive, a pinch of saffron adds a touch of royalty to dishes. So prized is it that it is at the centre of much trading fraud. The saffron you buy in the UK often comes from Iran and as there are a few grades available there, you can never be too sure of what you are getting! Your best bet is to buy from a reputed retailer, and make sure the box is tightly sealed. The saffron itself should be an even, deep red and slowly infuse milk with colour rather than turn it Day-Glo red straight away. Look out for British saffron, which is grown in Saffron Walden.

STAR ANISE CHAKRA PHOOL
Star anise is the aromatic fruit of the perennial anise tree and its Latin name is *illicium*, meaning 'alluring'. Liquorice-tinged allure is what it adds in plenty to pulao, biryani and meat curries.

TURMERIC HALDI
A cousin of the ginger root, turmeric offers colour and a host of health benefits, owing mostly to its curcumin content. It is available fresh or ground. I always have a supply of earthy fresh turmeric in my freezer, which I grate into porridge and blend with smoothies or milk. However, the warm and milder ground version is much better for cooking and marinades.

WHOLE DRIED RED CHILLIES LAL MIRCH
These can be sizzled whole (but without the stem) in hot oil to subtly infuse it with a kick. They are also used in ground form, adding heat and warmth to a recipe. Confusingly, the ground version is sometimes labelled as chilli powder, and sometimes as extra-hot chilli powder. My recipes assume the former.

From top:
Kashmiri chillies, whole dried red chillies, Indian green chillies

EXTENDED SPICE COLLECTION

This 'extended' spice collection features the ones that appear in only a few recipes. You can avoid buying them entirely unless such a recipe takes your fancy.

BENGALI FIVE-SPICE   PANCH PHORON
This classic five-spice mix, used in Bengali cooking and also in other parts of eastern India, has equal quantities of fenugreek, fennel, brown mustard, cumin and nigella seeds. It's great sizzled in hot oil with a dash of ginger and sautéed vegetables. Or in chutney!

CAROM SEEDS   AJWAIN
Combining the freshness of mint and the sharpness of thyme, carom seeds are well known for their digestive benefits and often just chewed on their own. Their spiky flavour is pitch-perfect for parathas, pakoras, bhajis and anything with gram flour, which can sometimes be difficult to digest.

FENUGREEK SEEDS   METHI
Lauded as a wonder spice, these sharp, bitter seeds of the methi plant may not be much to taste but have a ton of health properties and help move things along when preserving pickles and fermenting batters. When boiled in water they make a calming tea that aids digestion.

MANGO POWDER   AMCHOOR
Like garam masala, dried mango powder is added to recipes just before they finish cooking to add a tangy taste and distinctive aroma. You can substitute this with a squeeze of lemon or lime juice.

NIGELLA SEEDS   KALONJI
Often confused with black cumin seeds, nigella or black onion seeds have a characteristic musty flavour, like oregano spiked with onion. They make an excellent topping for naan, or can be sizzled in ghee as an alternative to cumin seeds in the tempering for a dal (page 149).

NUTMEG AND MACE   JAIPHAL AND JAVITRI
Nutmeg and mace are the seed and fibrous encasing of the *Myristica fragrans* fruit. Nutmeg has more of an affinity with sweet things, and both are a must in lavish aromatic dishes like lamb curry and biryani. Always buy them whole to retain their full floral impact.

WHITE PEPPER   SAFED MIRCHI
White pepper is the milder inner core of the black peppercorn. It is ground and used to add a more gentle hint of pepper to a dish without affecting its appearance. It is used mainly in creamy dishes with a white appearance, like a korma.

WHITE POPPY SEEDS   KHUS KHUS
Banned in many countries owing to their relation to the opium plant, nutritious white poppy seeds are used as a thickener for lavish curries, or in desserts and sweets. Fear not; the seeds themselves don't contain any psychoactive substances and can be used like any other spice.

Clockwise from top:
carom seeds, white poppy seeds, Bengali five-spice, white pepper, mace, mango powder, fenugreek seeds, nigella seeds.

Herbs and fresh ingredients like ginger, garlic and coconut play a key role in many spice pastes; they can also be used as a garnish.

COCONUT   NARIYAL
Nothing beats the taste of fresh coconut, so it is ever present in my home. My foolproof way of extracting the flesh is to give my kids a coconut each to chuck at the garden wall until the shell gives way. Poke a hole in the weakest dark spot on the coconut, then drain it over a bowl if you want to save the coconut water. Instead of destroying brick walls, you can also rigorously hammer the coconut all over, and then smash it, which loosens the flesh from the hard outer shell so that you can prise it out with a butter knife. Cut the flesh into 100g chunks, then put it in an airtight container and freeze for up to 2 months, if you like. To defrost take it out an hour before you need it.

Desiccated coconut is a passable substitute for the fresh variety, especially in chutneys and sweets. Soak the desiccated coconut in enough hot water to submerge it and then add a tablespoon of melted coconut oil for extra oomph. Conveniently, 100g soaked desiccated coconut is equivalent to the same amount of fresh coconut.

In India, the flesh of fresh coconut is blended, soaked and pressed to make coconut milk. The first press gives you thick milk, and the second press gives thin milk. However, tinned coconut milk is the most convenient option. Chose a good-quality brand that has at least 75 per cent coconut in it. Coconut milk powder is also a good alternative, which you can mix with water to your taste and preference.

CORIANDER   DHANIYA
The fresh floral flavour of coriander can be polarising, but I must confess I am a fan. Fresh is best for garnishing, but you can wash, dry and freeze it for marinades and chutneys. You can often use the soft stalks too, apart from the very thick bottom few centimetres of the bunch.

CURRY LEAVES   KARI PATTA
Citrusy, heady and irresistible, curry leaves spring to full fragrant effect when they are sizzled until crisp in hot oil. There is only one kind of curry leaf worth consuming and that's fresh; the dried varieties are perfumed parchment at best. Buy bags of the fresh stuff, wash, roughly dry the leaves on kitchen paper and freeze the leaves in airtight containers. Or better still, buy a plant online and grow it at home for a lifelong supply.

DILL   SUVA
Dill is not just for salmon! You can use it generously with roasted aubergine and also potatoes. It has a great affinity with turmeric and chilli powder. Like fresh coriander and mint, dill freezes well.

GINGER AND GARLIC   ADRAK AND LASAN
Ginger and garlic should always be peeled before use, and you can grate them finely with a Microplane grater (page 244) when using in recipes. You can also make batches of puréed ginger and garlic and freeze them in ice-cube trays. Two centimetres of ginger will yield one tablespoon when puréed; one fat garlic clove will yield one teaspoon. But I have discovered that making large batches of ginger-garlic paste is a thankless and laborious task that is best avoided unless you are blessed with an army of minions (progeny don't count). Whatever you do, please don't use ready-made jars of puréed garlic and ginger, except in an emergency, as they are simply not potent enough.

INDIAN GREEN CHILLIES   HARI MIRCH
Labelled as finger chillies in supermarkets and Indian green chillies in ethnic stores, these are thin, hot and full of fresh flavour, and are the ones used in my recipes. The spiciest bit is the membrane, not the seeds – please do not remove either unless the recipe demands it, as they are full of flavour. You can wash a stash of chillies and roughly dry, seal and freeze in bags for up to 2 months, or until the seeds turn brown.

These ingredients will help to add flavour to your cooking, especially as final flourishes.

LEMON AND LIME NIMBU

The lemons used in India are, in fact, limes — they are thin-skinned, yellow in colour and bursting with citrus juice. Compared to Indian limes, I find the key limes of Britain rather underwhelming so I prefer unwaxed organic lemons. Look out for Indian limes in ethnic stores.

MINT PUDINA

Fresh mint leaves work a treat in marinades and chutneys. Always strip the leaves from the stalks carefully, as errant stalks can turn the end result bitter. Like fresh coriander, you can wash, dry and freeze the leaves for up to 2 months. Frozen mint is best for marinades and chutneys, while fresh is best for raitas and as a garnish.

ONION PYAAZ

The red onions more commonly used in Indian cooking are smaller than their white counterparts and harder to source. I, therefore, use white onions for cooking and regular red for drenching with lemon juice and using as a garnish. Where shallots are called for, echalion or banana shallots are preferable as they are easier to peel.

PAPAYA ENZYME PAPAIN

Also known as meat tenderiser powder, papaya enzyme is a white powder that breaks down the fibres in meat. It's best used on barbecue meats as it helps the marinade penetrate the meat. Add it a couple of hours before cooking, as it's heat activated, and mix it in before seasoning, as it contains salt. Be warned: if you add too much too soon it will turn the meat into mush!

BLACK SALT KALA NAMAK

Onion-pink in colour, with a distinctive sulphuric fragrance like boiled eggs, black salt is processed volcanic rock salt. It has a great affinity with raita, street food and crispy nibbles. You can use any other mineral salt instead.

COCONUT VINEGAR TODDY

Used widely in Goa, coconut vinegar or *toddy* is also called palm vinegar and is available online, in health food stores or in your nearest ethnic supermarket. I prefer the cloudy unrefined version. If it's still a bit tricky to source, substitute cider vinegar.

JAGGERY GUR

Sticky, caramelly in taste and golden in hue, jaggery is unrefined sugar from the sugar cane plant. It comes tightly packed in a lump that you have to scrape at. As this can be laborious, feel free to use light or dark brown muscovado sugar instead.

ROSE WATER GULAB
SCREWPINE ESSENCE KEVDA (KEWRA)

A must-have for biryani-making — these two floral essences are guaranteed to transport you to the courts of the Mughal emperors.

TAMARIND IMLI

The tangy fruit and seeds of the tamarind tree are encased in a brown, dry pod. You can buy blocks of pressed tamarind pulp that you break off and infuse in hot water, then strain through a fine sieve, discarding the pulp; the infusion is then used as a souring agent. This works best for street food. For dal and curries, source a handy little tub of tamarind paste.

CONDIMENTS

While these are not strictly 'ingredients', papad, sev, pickle and chutney are used to dress a meal and so they earn their place here.

CHUTNEY

Authentic Indian chutney is a whole different beast from the congealed bottled stuff sold in the West. Our chutneys are usually made as needed with fresh or cooked ingredients, without the addition of vinegar for preservation. This is because the Raj-era British, who loved the taste of Indian chutneys, had to use acidic vinegar to make them when they returned to a motherland without the blazing sun we enjoy in India. We tend to blend raw fresh ingredients together or cook them down with sugar and then bottle the chutney to enjoy with meals. If buying ready-made chutneys, never double dip or expose them to moisture, as they will spoil.

LENTIL CRACKERS PAPAD

Papad are dried spiced lentil crackers whose crunch is the yin to the yang of mouthfuls of soft curry. They are commonly referred to in the West by their south Indian name 'pappadom' sometimes, annoyingly, with a fake Indian accent and shake of the head! Cook them in the microwave on high until evenly crisp or by turning quickly on an open flame until golden, charred and crisp. Interestingly, papad are usually bought rather than made at home: papad-making is now mostly limited to a few communities and regions, generally in rural areas. Some of my Marwari friends, who hail from Rajasthan, remember the ladies of the house coming together to make papad on their roof terraces; as it's women who make them, they are a symbol of female empowerment.

GRAM FLOUR NOODLES SEV

These crispy, spiced and deep-fried gram flour noodles make an excellent topping for street foods, salads and breakfasts and can be bought in large packs. You can enjoy sev on its own too as a punchy snack. Bombay mix is an acceptable stand-in.

PICKLE ACHAAR

Tart, tangy and spicy pickles add a little extra to every meal and I can't live without them. Making pickle is something of a dying art, even in India. Ethnic stores stock a dazzling array of pickles, although you have to work out which ones you like best through trial and error. There are two recipes in this book, however, on pages 222 and 223, that will not be easy to come by in the shops. Spoon the pickles sparingly onto your plate and remember, chutney-style rules apply to maintain their shelf life – always use a clean spoon – and no double dipping!

GRAINS AND FLOURS

Grains and flours provide the backbone of many Indian meals; only a small selection of the wide range used in India feature in this book.

CHAPPATI FLOUR CHAKKI ATTA
Ground in a stone mill called a *chakki*, atta is wholewheat durum flour. It is finely milled, in between plain flour and wholemeal, allowing for better absorption of moisture and a denser end product. My family are big fans of Pillsbury chakki atta. But there are lots of brands out there, so please do conduct your own trials.

FLATTENED RICE POHA
Poha is rice that is partially cooked, beaten and then dried, during which time it ferments and becomes flat, airy and soft. You just have to rehydrate it with a quick rinse in a sieve to bring it back to life. The fine version is used for breakfast cereal and fried snacks, while the medium (also called thick) version is better for savoury dishes. As it is probiotic, poha is used to aid the fermentation of batters used for south Indian Dosa (page 110).

GRAM FLOUR BESAN
This is Bengal gram or *chana dal* flour, often confusingly labelled chickpea flour. Bengal gram is a type of chickpea, but it isn't the one you're probably thinking of. This flour has a characteristic roasted-nut taste and a dense texture, which perfectly coats bhajis and pakoras, and also makes excellent gluten-free pancakes (page 95).

Eating raw besan is not a pleasant gastronomic experience, so please do make sure it is cooked before you eat it. Incidentally, it has vast uses in natural Indian skincare; my mother used it on us mixed into fresh whole milk cream as a body scrub until we were old enough to protest!

PUFFED RICE MURMURA (MAMRA)
'Puffed' rice is really just popped rice that is bagged up for snacking. It is enjoyed as a breakfast cereal, as an afternoon snack and in many street foods. Keep it well sealed as it does soften with time. Toast it briefly over a medium flame to help it regain its crispiness, adding peanuts, sev, salt and chilli to make a quick snack. If you can't find *mamra*, a bag of no-added-sugar/salt puffed rice cereal does the job.

RICE BASMATI
Always buy the very best long-grain rice you can for pulaos and biryanis, and follow the cooking method on page 162 for perfect results. If you're short on time, look out for pouches of ready-cooked rice, which make excellent fast food. While brown rice has wholesome goodness, it is chewy with curries and it takes an age to cook, so I stick to the white variety unless I am feeling particularly virtuous.

RICE FLOUR CHAWAL ATTA
Rice flour, made by grinding raw rice, was used to crisp up fried things, make pancakes and thicken dishes in India well before gluten became unfashionable. It is now readily available in most supermarkets.

SEMOLINA SOOJI (RAVA)
Semolina is used widely in India, both in sweet and savoury dishes. Waking up to heady curry-leaf-fragranced savoury semolina breakfasts used to be a weekend ritual in our family home. Importantly – and confusingly – you can buy coarse or fine semolina. If you don't fancy buying both just buy the coarse version and grind it fine.

PULSES

India has the highest percentage of vegetarianism in the world, mostly of the lacto-vegetarian kind (enjoying dairy but not eggs). Protein-rich pulses like lentils, therefore, form an important part of our diet. Importantly, lentils are sometimes used with their skins on (whole) and sometimes without (skinless and/or split) and need to be rinsed thoroughly and often soaked before use.

BENGAL GRAM (WHOLE)   KALA CHANA
These little Indian chickpeas, also known as brown chickpeas, have their skin intact and add crunch and a health injection to street food and snacking. There are three ways to use them: for speed you can buy them ready-cooked in tins; you can buy a bag of the raw whole Bengal gram to soak overnight and cook according to the packet instructions; or the third way is to sprout them (page 226).

BENGAL GRAM (SPLIT)   CHANA
The skinless split version of Bengal gram, *chana dal* is an earthy, nutty and comforting yellow lentil, mainly used for the thick dal favoured in Orissa and West Bengal. Like split pigeon peas, these take a while to cook. Don't confuse them with split yellow peas, which are *matar dal*, and not used in the recipes in this book.

BLACK GRAM (WHOLE)   URID (URAD)
Rich and nutty, black gram or whole *urid* lentils make excellent thick dals such as Ma Ki Dal (page 64). They do need soaking overnight before cooking.

BLACK GRAM (SKINLESS)   WHITE URID (URAD)
Black gram that has been split is white in colour, with no dark skin at all. With their powdery taste, these lentils mimic flour in fermented savoury dishes and are used to make spongy snacks and brunch treats.

GREEN MOONG BEANS   MOONG (MUNG)
Green moong beans are just yellow moong beans with the husk on, each sporting a little dent in its belly with a white pockmark on it. They need at least 3–4 hours of soaking.

RED SPLIT LENTILS   MASOOR DAL
Red split lentils cook quickly and turn into super-smooth dal with a mild flavour that's perfect for spiky spice tempering. You'll see them often in packets of 'soup mix' lentils.

SPLIT PIGEON PEAS   TOOR (ARHAR)
Toor or *arhar* dal is used extensively in Gujarati and south Indian cooking. It has a nutty flavour and retains its shape well, although it does take an age to cook. Buy the 'unoily' or 'dry' version and soak for an hour before using.

YELLOW LENTILS   MOONG (MUNG)
Yellow lentils are small with a warm nutty flavour that intensifies when dry-roasted. They cook quickly and don't need to be soaked.

Clockwise, from top left: Whole Bengal gram, split Bengal gram, yellow lentils, skinless black gram, red split lentils, split pigeon peas, whole black gram, green moong beans

DAIRY

Milk, cheese and yoghurt often form the base of our drinks, curries and desserts, as well as being served alongside meals in the form of a cooling raita.

FRESH INDIAN CHEESE PANEER
Paneer is available in handy vacuum-sealed blocks of pre-cut cubes, although I have given you a recipe for homemade paneer, if you're so inclined (page 225).

Always seal paneer in hot oil when you're using it for curries as it retains its shape better and allows the spices to infuse the cheese. However, don't bother if you're in a rush and don't mind the odd speck of crumbled paneer in your curry.

Importantly, paneer is not India's only cheese. The processed Amul cheese, which is sold in tins and cubes, is an Indian institution best known for its contribution to cheese toast (page 131) and its political-satire advertising. Medium Cheddar is a perfectly acceptable stand-in for it.

MILK POWDER KHOYA
Also known as *mawa*, this is milk that has been cooked until solid. It's an essential ingredient in desserts and sweet treats. Fresh *khoya* can be bought from specialist sweet shops, but it is available more conveniently as milk powder. Store in an airtight container once open.

YOGHURT DAHI
Yoghurt is often used to thicken curries. To prevent curdling, always use full-fat Greek-style yoghurt, as opposed to lower fat varieties, and make sure it is at room temperature. Give it a good whisk before adding it to the pan and briefly take the pan off direct heat when you stir in the yoghurt.

MEAT AND FISH

Meat curries in India are primarily made of goat, which is also referred to as mutton in India (as is lamb meat). I use lamb in this book, as it is easier to source. You can also use chunks of stewing beef.

For meat curries that are cooked for substantial amounts of time, I would recommend using meat on the bone to get the full impact of highly nutritious stock in your dish, unless otherwise specified in the recipe. Look out for lamb fore shanks and leg shanks, as you can combine these with diced neck fillet to make a supermarket-ingredient-friendly curry. For chicken curries, use thighs and drumsticks only — chicken breasts are virtually impenetrable to spices!

While I wouldn't propose you stockpile factory-farmed meat, remember that slow-cooking and an abundance of spices means you don't need to splurge on choice cuts. If you do head to the butcher, diced on-the-bone lamb shoulder is better value than leg and just as meltingly soft when stewed.

With fish curries, opt for firm-fleshed varieties like hake, monkfish, tilapia and swordfish that won't flake when handled. Check with your fishmonger or the packet instructions for advice on how to store and use. Supermarket bags of sustainable frozen fish are also convenient for Fishcakes (page 134), Kedgeree (page 114) and dishes like Meen Curry (page 50).

Similarly, bags of sustainable frozen raw king prawns are great for everyday cooking, and defrost quickly when dunked in cold water. Blow the budget with extra large raw king prawns sourced from a fishmonger if you want to impress. Clean the prawns by slitting the back with the tip of a sharp knife and removing the dark vein (digestive tract).

OIL

Watching a little oil float to the surface of an Indian curry is a happy sign that the ingredients are well cooked and beautifully incorporated. The oil used depends on which region the dish is from and how it tastes.

COCONUT OIL

Always buy raw extra-virgin coconut oil, which solidifies at room temperature and has a strong flavour and plenty of goodness. Pack it into your measuring spoon in its solid state when measuring for recipes. Until coconut oil is scientifically proven to be an elixir for immortal youth, I am not prepared to make everything taste of coconuts by using it as a replacement for neutral oil.

GHEE

Though similar to clarified butter, ghee is even more pure and is usually just used to infuse a recipe with flavour, or sometimes as a finishing touch. However, celebrity Indian nutritionist and author Rujuta Diwekar recommends deep-frying in homemade ghee, backed by strong scientific evidence on its healing, fat burning and GI-reducing properties.

Like coconut oil, ghee comes packed solid in a tin, so simply pile it into your measuring spoon solid. You will find a cheat's recipe for proper homemade ghee on page 224. As I am not yet at the regular ghee-making stage of my life I generally just buy an Indian brand instead.

MUSTARD OIL

Mustard oil has a warm and pungent taste and is a great base for pickles too. Outside India it is sometimes sold with an alarming label that declares 'unfit for internal consumption'. The sticking point is inconclusive scientific evidence on the effects of erucic acid under certain lab conditions. Mercifully we are not lab rats, and this oil boasts a number of health benefits that make it grandma's favourite grease and a staple for cooking, body massages and hair and skin conditioning. Grab a bottle of the blended version if you're still concerned.

NEUTRAL OIL

Unless otherwise specified, the oil used to cook Indian food is flavourless, neutral oil. Sunflower and corn oils are my preferred choice; refined rapeseed oil (often labelled as 'vegetable oil') is also a good option.

EQUIPMENT

Many gadgets and utensils that you already have in your kitchen can be put to excellent use for Indian cooking.

KITCHEN GADGETS

You can achieve much with a sharp knife and a wooden spatula when it comes to Indian cooking, but appliances do simplify life. These are my top buys.

HAND BLENDER

This little gadget packs a big punch. You can make smaller quantities of smooth masala pastes and chutney in the chopper attachment, purée your own ginger and garlic, and use the wand attachment to go straight into your pan to blend ingredients into super-smooth, restaurant-style curries. If you're buying a new one, pick a 'turbo' 1000-watt version and look for a multitasker that comes with food processor attachments.

HIGH-SPEED BLENDER OR SMOOTHIE MAKER

A powerful blender, the kind you make smoothies in, is a great tool that helps you whip up larger quantities of smooth pancake and crepe batters in no time at all. You can always use your hand blender's chopper attachment in batches too if you prefer. If you're worried about spice aromas lingering, see my troubleshooting tips on page 247.

ELECTRIC COFFEE GRINDER

An inexpensive coffee grinder doubles up as an excellent spice grinder for making small quantities of your own garam masala and roasted ground cumin, as long as you don't use the same one for both! The one with a removable bowl is best for cleaning. I much prefer it to a pestle and mortar, which takes longer and inevitably involves specks of spices flying in my face.

PESTLE AND MORTAR

Despite my flagrant dismissal of this gadget, above, it does have its uses. Reach for this when you need to crush smaller quantities of spices and control their texture.

MICROPLANE GRATER

This is the fine, flat-sided grater that turns the hardest of ingredients, like chocolate and nutmeg, into shavings of dust in no time. Ginger and garlic are easy to finely grate directly into a bubbling, steaming pot without the need for a multi-piece gadget. Buy the sharpest one you can find and keep your fingers and nails safe from harm's way.

SPRING-LOADED ICE CREAM SCOOP
This may appear to be a curious gadget for an Indian cookbook. A spring-loaded ice cream scoop is an ingenius tool that allows you to evenly measure portions of dough, batter and other ingredients for cooking. If, like me, you're not very good at judging quantities by eye, then using one of these will give you perfectly even kebabs, parathas, pakoras… the list goes on. A small one is good for desserts, while the larger size is great for bhajis and kebabs.

HEAVY-DUTY FOOD PROCESSOR
This is the kind that sits on your worktop and requires elbow grease to move. It's not essential but it chops, slices, blends, shreds, grates and even makes you a cup of tea if you treat it well enough. Maybe not the latter, but the plethora of tasks this baby can perform means you'll have ample time to make that cup of tea. You can get by with a Microplane grater, mandoline and sharp knife if you don't have this at home but it's worth the investment if you're hoping to make large quantities of shredded and grated dishes.

Of all the material goods I possess, I am definitely most protective of my pots and pans. Good-quality heavy-based non-stick pans are best. These sturdy items will make a breeze of caramelising onions, transforming spices and cooking spice pastes.

The best approach to building a collection of hard-wearing pots and pans is to buy eye-wateringly expensive, semi-professional ones, one at a time, and spend time and energy looking after them. Never put them in a dishwasher, store them one on top of each other without protective dividers, or use metal cooking spoons.

Well-seasoned iron flat griddles are also great for Indian cooking if you have a gas hob – especially with dosa and other crepes or pancakes. Look for traditional ones in Indian shops. Before using one for the first time, wash it well, heat until smoking, swirl with oil and then carefully wipe with kitchen paper. Repeat three times. The edges will crust beautifully over time – this is par for the course.

While you may not need specialist utensils to cook Indian food, it's useful to know what they are.

HANDI (PRONOUNCED *HUN-DEE*)
A wide-mouthed, deep pot with a neck near the top. It is used for *dum*, or slow-cooking. You can use a deep casserole dish with a tight-fitting lid.

KADAI (PRONOUNCED *KER-HAI*)
Shaped like a wok, but deeper and with steeper sides. (A wok is a perfectly acceptable substitute.)

TADKA PAN (PRONOUNCED *TER-KA*)
A little round *kadai* that is perfect for tempering spices. You can use an egg pan, but unveiling a dinky tadka pan is one of my favourite party tricks.

TAWA (PRONOUNCED *TUV-VA*)
A flat round pan with a slightly concave base. The shape is perfect for flatbreads and pancakes. You can use a seasoned round flat griddle instead.

TROUBLESHOOTING

Rule Number One with Indian cooking is to keep an eye out for changing texture, taste and even colour. Rule Number Two is never to try a new recipe when guests are waiting to be fed. If things still go awry, here are some simple fixes.

TIPS FOR COOKING

SPICES SMELL FUSTY

Don't throw them out! Warm old spices briefly in a medium-hot pan to reinvigorate them and then use as normal. The lesson here: cook more Indian food!

MISSING AN INGREDIENT

If it's a minor ingredient you can leave it out and no one will be any the wiser. Although you obviously didn't hear this from me.

NO TIME TO MARINATE MEAT

No drama. Use papaya enzyme, or meat tenderiser powder (page 237).

ONIONS NOT TURNING GOLDEN

Add another tablespoon of the base cooking oil used in the recipe, a pinch of sugar and salt and keep going.

SPICES CATCHING ON THE BOTTOM OF THE PAN

If your pan runs out of moisture, the spices will catch on the bottom of the pan. If they do, add a little hot water and scrape off. If they're completely burnt, see below.

SPICES OR MASALA BURNT

Skim off the unburnt bits from the top and continue in a fresh pan. If the entire lot is burnt, simply start again. There's no point crying over burnt spices.

TOO MUCH SALT

Add a bit more of the key base ingredient of your curry: yoghurt, tomato, coconut milk, etc. A dash of cream or squirt of lemon juice also works wonders.

TOO MUCH WATER

Whack the heat up and bubble any excess moisture away. You may want to set aside the meat, fish or vegetables in the dish first so they don't overcook.

YOGHURT HAS SPLIT

Keep cooking the dish until it's done. Scoop out the vegetables or meat and any whole spices from the dish and set them aside. Use a hand blender to process the rest into a smooth curry, then pop everything back in the pan. Pray no one will notice, and then reread my tips on cooking with yoghurt on page 242.

DAL NOT COOKING

Add hot water, cover and cook, stirring from time to time. Remember, adding cold water to dal or any food while it's cooking will slow things down.

CURRY OR DAL TOO DRY

Loosen the contents with half a cup of water or more, depending on how much fluid you want. Curry and lentils both dry out as they sit around so just adjust the liquid before you serve.

CURRY HAS A BITTER AFTERTASTE

Did you add the garam masala, fenugreek or mango powder too early? Add salt, sugar or tomatoes to balance out the bitterness.

ENTIRE HOME SMELLS OF CURRY

Keep the kitchen door closed and the window open or fan on when you cook. Light a scented candle after you have finished cooking, or incense if you can bear it.

ODOUR IN BLENDER

Fill your blender with a solution of one part vinegar to two parts warm water then leave to soak overnight. Blend in the morning before proceeding to clean as usual, dry and then store away.

TURMERIC STAINS

There is no stain that bicarbonate of soda doesn't resolve. If your worktop or clothes are stained at home, make a thick paste of the soda with water and leave to treat the area for 15–30 minutes before washing off with your usual cleaner. For stained fingernails, coat them in cooking oil (as turmeric is oil-soluble) then use washing up liquid and a nail brush to remove the stains.

GARLIC FINGERNAILS

Hold a butter knife under cold water in the kitchen sink and slowly massage the flat side onto the affected digits and voila! – say goodbye to garlicky fingernails. Don't ask me how it works, it just does!

INDEX

A THOUSAND THANKS

Saying thanks to the near and dear is considered too formal in India, but I'm going to do it anyway.

Ann Mah, Steve Rhinds and Jules Gilbert for their early insights. Ione Walder for cheering me on. Kate Lough at the Evening Standard for taking a chance on me, and Jen Stebbing for the opportunity and constant support.

My literary agent and wise owl Claire Conrad, for never giving up on me, and the fantastic team at Janklow & Nesbit.

Richard Atkinson and Natalie Bellos for spotting a little something in the book proposal. Xa Shaw Stewart, my editor and constant one, for endless patience, creativity and energy. The sage Lisa Pendreigh for getting it over the line and Lena Hall for ably supporting everything.

Issy Croker for beautiful photography and love of chai and all things India. Steph McLeod for limitless enthusiasm, and jumpers. Bloody clever girl Emily Ezekiel for recipe and styling creativity. Kitty Coles for hard graft in the kitchen and around the streets of Tooting.

Designer Sandra Zellmer for thoughtfulness and deep consideration – you are a blessing! Copy-editor Clare Sayer – your expert eye would put most eagles to shame.

My lucky mascot, Chief Recipe Officer and firm friend Devika Jhala aka Boobie. My Begum Pooja Vir for top advice, a hungry belly and unfailing support. Priyankaa and the Vir family, my wonderful hosts in Hyderabad. Oli Watts and Sara Wallace for the company and capturing beautiful memories.

To all the chefs and seasoned cooks who welcomed me into their restaurants and homes in Hyderabad and Vizag – Arundati Rao, Hema Aunty, Yasser and family, Krishna Aunty, Indira Aunty, Khalil Ahmed, Chef Challapathy Rao, Chef Sajesh and Chef Emon. Chef Abhishek Kukreti for the fish market trip and cooking demo at Chef Murli's home – it was amazing-zing-zing!

Experience Travel Group for organising my trip to Kerala – especially Sara, Sam and the much tormented Sinna. Chef Manoj of Brunton Boatyard, Chef Naveen and George and Sumi of Villa De Parayil. Filmmaker and childhood bestie Alka for joining the ride – you are the cheapest and best form of therapy.

Debashishda of Oh Calcutta, Ramani of 6 Ballygunge Place, Ifte of Calcutta Walks, Monica Aunty of Beijing and Sid of Mocambo for the special taste of Calcutta. Jennydi and Byju for food love and networks.

Friends who have weighed in with recipe tasting, ideas and more – Sanchita Paul, Kailas and Jeetu Patel, Adam and Sophie Papa, Sally and Graham Hishmurgh, Linda Griffin, Craig Westwood, Simon Folley, Louise Fernley, Iqbal Wahhab, Daniel Sharp, Shujoya Venugopalan, Lesley Katon and Tim Rich, Liam and Sam Walker, Lisa and Jon Aylward, and many more named throughout this book.

Oliver Jones for sound advice and YouTube adventures.

Catherine Arnold for guidance on my personal health and nutrition – you inspired so many recipes in here.

Mark Gallagher, Oli Foster, Grainne Warner and Sara Price for giving me a chance to pursue my dreams – you run the best communication consultancy. The incredible folk of Pagefield – you are a credit to the industry. Thanks to Kate Levine for introducing us.

Chiki Sarkar, Hugh Fraser and Jenny Heller for kickstarting my food writing journey. Everyone who has cooked my recipes, shared kind words and advice since.

And finally my family, without whom I am nothing.

Mother for relentless recipe advice, food and family history. You are my rock and an inspiration with your fuchsia-pink sarees and white hair.

Andres Reynaga, my husband, critical friend and branding guru, for braving the recipe fails and meltdowns. My darling children – kitchen helpers and recipe testers extraordinaire.

The Basu sisters. My middle sister Juthika and Brother-in-Law No. 1, Devdutta, for help with my India travels and recipe inputs. My little sister Bithika and Brother-in-Law No. 2, Tridib, for eager taste testing.

Dadu, my granddad for an extraordinary childhood – I appreciate you more every day.

My dad, nani and aunt, Dolly Pishi, for all the fabulous food memories and stories. I almost certainly inherited this mad passion from you!

BLOOMSBURY PUBLISHING
Bloomsbury Publishing Plc
50 Bedford Square, London, WC1B 3DP, UK

BLOOMSBURY, BLOOMSBURY PUBLISHING and the Diana logo
are trademarks of Bloomsbury Publishing Plc

First published in Great Britain 2018

A catalogue record for this book is available from the British Library

ISBN: HB: 978-1-4088-8688-5; eBook: 978-1-4088-8687-8

10 9 8 7 6 5 4 3 2 1

Project Editor: Clare Sayer
Designer: Sandra Zellmer
Photographer: Issy Croker
Food and Prop Stylist: Emily Ezekiel
Indexer: Hilary Bird

Printed and bound in China by RR Donnelley APS

Bloomsbury Publishing Plc makes every effort to ensure that
the papers used in the manufacture of our books are natural,
recyclable products made from wood grown in well-managed
forests. Our manufacturing processes conform to the
environmental regulations of the country of origin.

To find out more about our authors and books visit
www.bloomsbury.com and sign up for our newsletters